ROYAL COURT

Royal Court Theatre presents

FOOD CHAIN

by **Mick Mahoney**

First performance at the Royal Court Jerwood Theatre Upstairs
Sloane Square, London on 19 June 2003.

Supported by Jerwood New Playwrights

JERWOOD
NEW PLAYWRIGHTS

FOOD CHAIN

by **Mick Mahoney**

Cast in order of appearance
Billy **Calum Callaghan**
Jamie **Sid Mitchell**
Carol **Linda Robson**
Emma **Claire Rushbrook**
Tony **Paul Ritter**
Nat **Justin Salinger**

Director **Anna Mackmin**
Designer **Ti Green**
Lighting Designer **Johanna Town**
Sound Designer **Emma Laxton**
Casting Director **Lisa Makin**
Production Manager **Sue Bird**
Stage Management **Tamara Albachari**, **Maxine Foo**
Stage Management Work Placement **Hirohiko Ejiri**
Costume Supervisor **Kathryn Waters**
Fight Director **Terry King**
Choreographer **Scarlett Mackmin**

The Royal Court Theatre would like to thank the following for their help with this production:
Nintendo, Safeway, Sainsbury's, Waitrose, Walkers Snack Food Ltd.

THE COMPANY

Mick Mahoney (writer)
For the Royal Court: Sacred Heart (& RNT Studio).
Other theatre includes: Swaggers, Fantasy Bonds,
Too Many Films (Old Red Lion); Friday Nights (Old
Red Lion/Riverside); Shift (RNT Studio/Old Red
Lion); Street Trash, Sharon & Yassa, Rucker's Touch,
Up for None (RNT Studio); When Your Bottle's
Gone in SE1 (Soho Poly).
Television includes: Saracen, The Council.
Film includes: The Last Resort, Only a Fortnight,
Gangsterlene, Hero of the Underworld.
Awards include: 1999 Time Out Award for Best
Play for Swaggers, Verity Bargate Award for Up for
None, Thames Television Bursary.

Calum Callaghan
Theatre includes: Whistle Down the Wind
(Aldwych/Sydmonton Festival); Oliver! (London
Palladium); Les Miserables (London Palace); Hey Mr
Producer (Lyceum).
Television includes: Wall of Silence, The Bill, The
Tiny Living Channel, Stitch Up, Rat Boy, Gypsy Girl,
Writing & Pictures, Black Hearts in Battersea,
Children in Need, Hale & Pace, Ant & Dec.
Film includes: Love, Honour & Obey.

Ti Green (designer)
Theatre includes: Comedy of Errors (forthcoming
production at Bristol Old Vic); Dimetos, Epitaph for
the Whales, The Birds (Gate); Where There's a Will
(Peter Hall Company); Coriolanus (The Swan,
RSC/regional & US tour/Old Vic); Full House/The
Hairless Diva (Watford Palace); The Taming of the
Shrew (Nottingham Playhouse); The Christmas
Carol, Oedipus, Treasure Island, The Tempest, The
Wind in the Willows, Twelfth Night (Nuffield,
Southampton); Bogus Woman (Bush/Plymouth
Drum/national tour/Red Room/Traverse); Memory
of Water (English Speaking Theatre of Vienna); The
John Wayne Principle (Pleasance/Nuffield,
Southampton); Macbeth, Albertine in Five Times
(BAC); The Three Sisters (Oxford Stage Company/
Whitehall/tour); The Winter's Tale (British Council
co-production with Gavella Theatre, Zagreb);
Macbeth, Bodies, Simpleton of the Unexpected
Isles, Retreat (Orange Tree, Richmond); Obsession
(The Red Room/Etcetera/BAC); Just the Three of
Us (Theatre Royal, Windsor).
Television includes: On a Life's Edge.
Film includes: Saved.
Opera includes: The Barber of Seville (Grange Park
Opera), The Threepenny Opera (Pimlico Opera).

Emma Laxton (sound designer)
As sound designer, for the Royal Court:
Terrorism.
Other theatre includes: As You Like It, Romeo
and Juliet (Regent's Park Open Air Theatre).
Emma is Sound Deputy at the Royal Court.

Anna Mackmin (director)
Theatre includes: Air Swimming (BAC); In
Flame (Bush/West End); Memory of Water
(Vienna); The Arbor, Teeth 'n' Smiles,
Iphigenia (Sheffield Crucible); Auntie & Me
(Gaiety, Dublin/Wyndhams/Assembly Rooms,
Edinburgh Festival).
Anna is Literary Associate at the Sheffield
Crucible.

Sid Mitchell
For the Royal Court: Lift Off.
Theatre includes: Playing Fields (Soho); Sing
Yer Heart Out for the Lads (RNT); The Dead
Eye Boy (Hampstead); Lulu (Almeida/Kennedy
Center, Washington); Oliver! (Palladium);
Swan Lake (Sadler's Wells).
Television includes: Odd Socks, Henry VIII,
Ready When You Are, Mr McGill, Holby City,
Sunburn, Summer in the Suburbs, Small
Potatoes, The Bill, London's Burning.
Film includes: The Invitation, Goodbye Charlie
Bright.
Awards include: Olivier Award Nominee for
Most Promising Performance for The Dead
Eye Boy.
Radio includes: Tell Tale, Diggers.

Paul Ritter
For the Royal Court: The Night Heron,
Bluebird.
Other theatre includes: Accidental Death of
an Anarchist (Donmar); The Coast of Utopia,
Howard Katz, Remembrance of Things Past,
All My Sons (RNT); Troilus and Cressida,
Three Sisters (Oxford Stage Company);
Drummers (Out of Joint).
Television includes: Peterloo, Fields of Gold,
Big Cat, Out of Hours, The Bill, National
Achievement Day, Seaforth, Small Change.
Film includes: The Nine Lives of Tomas Katz,
Esther Kahn, Joy Rider.

Linda Robson

Theatre includes: Passionate Woman (Australia tour); Leaving (Soho Poly).
Television includes: Shine on Harvey Moon, Harry's Game, Birds of a Feather, Jobs for the Girls, Renovation Street, Hogwash, The Bill, The Helper, Crossroads, Home of their Own, Mary's Wife, Ain't Many Angels, Kate-The Good Neighbour, If Only, Chains, L for Lester, Lizzie's Pictures, Bad Boyes, Thin Air, South of the Border, Underground, Civvystreet, Cribb, Going Out, Agony, The Other Arf, The Case of the Middle-Aged Wife, Harry's Game, Elphida.
Radio includes: An Office Rumour.

Claire Rushbrook

For the Royal Court: Hated Nightfall (& tour).
Other theatre includes: Worlds Apart (Theatre Royal Stratford East); The Crucible (Sheffield Crucible); Richard II, Hindle Wakes (Royal Exchange, Manchester); Good Natur'd Man (Orange Tree, Richmond); Raising Fires (Bush); Uncle Vanya (Almeida/tour); Three Sisters (Oxford Stage Company/tour/West End); Fifty Revolutions (Whitehall).
Television includes: Casualty, The Turning World, Touching Evil, Coronation Street, He Can't Stop Here, Spaced, The Visitor, The Sins, Stretford Wives, Linda Green.
Film includes: Secrets and Lies, Crocodile Snap, Under the Skin, Spiceworld, Plunkett and Macleane, Shiner, Dr Sleep, A Changed Man, Tethered, Mary and Mick.

Justin Salinger

For the Royal Court: Under the Blue Sky.
Other theatre includes: Modern Dance for Beginners (Soho); Kick for Touch (Sheffield Crucible); Privates on Parade (Donmar); Iphigenia (Abbey, Dublin); Jump Mr Malinoff (Soho); The Backroom (Bush); Perpetua (Birmingham Rep); Peter Pan, Chips with Everything, Dealer's Choice (RNT); Much Ado about Nothing (Cheek by Jowl); Candide (Gate); Dona Rosita the Spinster (Almeida); Salome (RNT Studio).
Television includes: Foyle's War, Hitler: The Rise of Evil, Murphy's Law, Trust, Waking the Dead, Offenders, The Great Dome Robbery, The Vice, Dark Realm, The Bill, London's Burning.
Film includes: Revenger's Tragedy, Peaches, Velvet Goldmine.

Johanna Town (lighting designer)

Johanna has been Head of Lighting at the Royal Court Theatre, London since 1990, during which time she has lit over 30 productions for the company. Most recent shows include: Under the Whaleback and Terrorism.
Johanna's freelance career has taken her all over the world having designed the lighting for over 100 productions from London's West End to the far ends of Australasia.
Other lighting designs for 2003 include: She Stoops to Conquer/A Laughing Matter (Out Of Joint/RNT), Brassed Off (Liverpool Playhouse/Birmingham Rep), Mr Nobody (Soho Theatre).

ROYAL COURT
JERWOOD THEATRE DOWNSTAIRS

12 June - 12 July 2003
FALLOUT
by Roy Williams

A boy is found dead. D.C. Joe Stephens must return to his old neighbourhood to investigate. Shanice is avoiding his questions about her boyfriend, Emile, and his mates. Ronnie saw something, but promised Shanice she'd say nothing. But when a reward is offered, keeping quiet becomes a major test of their street loyalty.

Direction **Ian Rickson**
Design **Ultz**
Sound **Ian Dickinson**
Music **Stephen Warbeck**

Cast **Lorraine Brunning, O-T Fagbenle, Lennie James, Petra Letang, Marcel McCalla, Michael Obiora, Daniel Ryan, Ony Uhiara, Clive Wedderburn.**

Supported by Jerwood New Playwrights

Box Office 020 7565 5000
www.royalcourttheatre.com

THE ENGLISH STAGE COMPANY
AT THE ROYAL COURT

The English Stage Company at the Royal Court
opened in 1956 as a subsidised theatre
producing new British plays, international plays
and some classical revivals.

The first artistic director George Devine aimed
to create a writers' theatre, 'a place where the
dramatist is acknowledged as the fundamental
creative force in the theatre and where the play
is more important than the actors, the director,
the designer'. The urgent need was to find a
contemporary style in which the play, the acting,
direction and design are all combined. He
believed that 'the battle will be a long one to
continue to create the right conditions for
writers to work in'.

Devine aimed to discover 'hard-hitting,
uncompromising writers whose plays are
stimulating, provocative and exciting'. The Royal
Court production of John Osborne's Look Back
in Anger in May 1956 is now seen as the decisive
starting point of modern British drama and the
policy created a new generation of British
playwrights. The first wave included John
Osborne, Arnold Wesker, John Arden, Ann
Jellicoe, N F Simpson and Edward Bond. Early
seasons included new international plays by
Bertolt Brecht, Eugène Ionesco, Samuel Beckett,
Jean-Paul Sartre and Marguerite Duras.

The theatre started with the 400-seat
proscenium arch Theatre Downstairs, and then
in 1969 opened a second theatre, the 60-seat
studio Theatre Upstairs. Some productions
transfer to the West End, such as Terry Johnson's
Hitchcock Blonde, Caryl Churchill's Far Away,
Conor McPherson's The Weir, Kevin Elyot's
Mouth to Mouth and My Night With Reg. The
Royal Court also co-produces plays which have
transferred to the West End or toured interna-
tionally, such as Sebastian Barry's The Steward of
Christendom and Mark Ravenhill's Shopping and
Fucking (with Out of Joint), Martin McDonagh's
The Beauty Queen Of Leenane (with Druid
Theatre Company), Ayub Khan-Din's East is East
(with Tamasha Theatre Company, and now a
feature film).

Since 1994 the Royal Court's artistic policy has
again been vigorously directed to finding and
producing a new generation of playwrights. The
writers include Joe Penhall, Rebecca Prichard,
Michael Wynne, Nick Grosso, Judy Upton,
Meredith Oakes, Sarah Kane, Anthony Neilson,
Judith Johnson, James Stock, Jez Butterworth,
Marina Carr, Phyllis Nagy, Simon Block, Martin
McDonagh, Mark Ravenhill, Ayub Khan-Din,
Tamantha Hammerschlag, Jess Walters, Ché
Walker, Conor McPherson, Simon Stephens,

photo: Andy Chopping

Richard Bean, Roy Williams, Gary Mitchell, Mick
Mahoney, Rebecca Gilman, Christopher Shinn,
Kia Corthron, David Gieselmann, Marius von
Mayenburg, David Eldridge, Leo Butler, Zinnie
Harris, Grae Cleugh, Roland Schimmelpfennig,
DeObia Oparei, Vassily Sigarev and The
Presnyakov Brothers. This expanded programme
of new plays has been made possible through
the support of A.S.K Theater Projects and the
Skirball Foundation, the Jerwood Charitable
Foundation, the American Friends of the Royal
Court Theatre and many in association with the
Royal National Theatre Studio.

In recent years there have been record-breaking
productions at the box office, with capacity
houses for Terry Johnson's Hitchcock Blonde,
Caryl Churchill's A Number, Jez Butterworth's
The Night Heron, Rebecca Gilman's Boy Gets
Girl, Kevin Elyot's Mouth To Mouth, David
Hare's My Zinc Bed and Conor McPherson's
The Weir, which transferred to the West End in
October 1998 and ran for nearly two years at
the Duke of York's Theatre.

The newly refurbished theatre in Sloane Square
opened in February 2000, with a policy still
inspired by the first artistic director George
Devine. The Royal Court is an international
theatre for new plays and new playwrights, and
the work shapes contemporary drama in Britain
and overseas.

AWARDS FOR
THE ROYAL COURT

Jez Butterworth won the 1995 George Devine Award, the Writers' Guild New Writer of the Year Award, the Evening Standard Award for Most Promising Playwright and the Olivier Award for Best Comedy for Mojo.

The Royal Court was the overall winner of the 1995 Prudential Award for the Arts for creativity, excellence, innovation and accessibility. The Royal Court Theatre Upstairs won the 1995 Peter Brook Empty Space Award for innovation and excellence in theatre.

Michael Wynne won the 1996 Meyer-Whitworth Award for The Knocky. Martin McDonagh won the 1996 George Devine Award, the 1996 Writers' Guild Best Fringe Play Award, the 1996 Critics' Circle Award and the 1996 Evening Standard Award for Most Promising Playwright for The Beauty Queen of Leenane. Marina Carr won the 19th Susan Smith Blackburn Prize (1996/7) for Portia Coughlan. Conor McPherson won the 1997 George Devine Award, the 1997 Critics' Circle Award and the 1997 Evening Standard Award for Most Promising Playwright for The Weir. Ayub Khan-Din won the 1997 Writers' Guild Awards for Best West End Play and Writers' Guild New Writer of the Year and the 1996 John Whiting Award for East is East (co-production with Tamasha).

At the 1998 Tony Awards, Martin McDonagh's The Beauty Queen of Leenane (co-production with Druid Theatre Company) won four awards including Garry Hynes for Best Director and was nominated for a further two. Eugene Ionesco's The Chairs (co-production with Theatre de Complicite) was nominated for six Tony awards. David Hare won the 1998 Time Out Live Award for Outstanding Achievement and six awards in New York including the Drama League, Drama Desk and New York Critics Circle Award for Via Dolorosa. Sarah Kane won the 1998 Arts Foundation Fellowship in Playwriting. Rebecca Prichard won the 1998 Critics' Circle Award for Most Promising Playwright for Yard Gal (co-production with Clean Break).

Conor McPherson won the 1999 Olivier Award for Best New Play for The Weir. The Royal Court won the 1999 ITI Award for Excellence in International Theatre. Sarah Kane's Cleansed was judged Best Foreign Language Play in 1999 by Theater Heute in Germany. Gary Mitchell won the 1999 Pearson Best Play Award for Trust. Rebecca Gilman was joint winner of the 1999 George Devine Award and won the 1999 Evening Standard Award for Most Promising Playwright for The Glory of Living.

In 1999, the Royal Court won the European theatre prize New Theatrical Realities, presented at Taormina Arte in Sicily, for its efforts in recent years in discovering and producing the work of young British dramatists.

Roy Williams and Gary Mitchell were joint winners of the George Devine Award 2000 for Most Promising Playwright for Lift Off and The Force of Change respectively. At the Barclays Theatre Awards 2000 presented by the TMA, Richard Wilson won the Best Director Award for David Gieselmann's Mr Kolpert and Jeremy Herbert won the Best Designer Award for Sarah Kane's 4.48 Psychosis. Gary Mitchell won the Evening Standard's Charles Wintour Award 2000 for Most Promising Playwright for The Force of Change. Stephen Jeffreys' I Just Stopped by to See The Man won an AT&T: On Stage Award 2000.

David Eldridge's Under the Blue Sky won the Time Out Live Award 2001 for Best New Play in the West End. Leo Butler won the George Devine Award 2001 for Most Promising Playwright for Redundant. Roy Williams won the Evening Standard's Charles Wintour Award 2001 for Most Promising Playwright for Clubland. Grae Cleugh won the 2001 Olivier Award for Most Promising Playwright for Fucking Games. Richard Bean was joint winner of the George Devine Award 2002 for Most Promising Playwright for Under the Whaleback. Caryl Churchill won the 2002 Evening Standard Award for Best New Play for A Number. Vassily Sigarev won the 2002 Evening Standard Charles Wintour Award for Most Promising Playwright for Plasticine. Ian MacNeil won the 2002 Evening Standard Award for Best Design for A Number and Plasticine. Peter Gill won the 2002 Critics' Circle Award for Best New Play for The York Realist (English Touring Theatre).

ROYAL COURT BOOKSHOP

The bookshop offers a wide range of playtexts and theatre books, with over 1,000 titles. Located in the downstairs Bar and Food area, the bookshop is open Monday to Saturday, afternoons and evenings.

Many Royal Court playtexts are available for just £2 including works by Harold Pinter, Caryl Churchill, Rebecca Gilman, Martin Crimp, Sarah Kane, Conor McPherson, Ayub Khan-Din, Timberlake Wertenbaker and Roy Williams.

For information on titles and special events, Email: bookshop@royalcourttheatre.com
Tel: 020 7565 5024

PROGRAMME SUPPORTERS

The Royal Court (English Stage Company Ltd) receives its principal funding from London Arts. It is also supported financially by a wide range of private companies and public bodies and earns the remainder of its income from the box office and its own trading activities.
The Royal Borough of Kensington & Chelsea gives an annual grant to the Royal Court Young Writers' Programme.

The Jerwood Charitable Foundation continues to support new plays by new playwrights through the Jerwood New Playwrights series. Since 1993 A.S.K. Theater Projects and the Skirball Foundation have funded a Playwrights' Programme at the theatre. Bloomberg Mondays, the Royal Court's reduced price ticket scheme, is supported by Bloomberg. Over the past seven years the BBC has supported the Gerald Chapman Fund for directors.

ROYAL COURT DEVELOPMENT BOARD
Tamara Ingram (Chair)
Jonathan Cameron (Vice Chair)
Timothy Burrill
Anthony Burton
Jonathan Caplan QC
Sindy Caplan
Joseph Fiennes
Kimberly Fortier
Joyce Hytner
Dan Klein
Gavin Neath
Michael Potter
Ben Rauch
Kadee Robbins
Mark Robinson
William Russell
Sue Stapely
James L Tanner
Will Turner

TRUSTS AND FOUNDATIONS
American Friends of the Royal Court Theatre
The Carnegie United Kingdom Trust
Carlton Television Trust
Gerald Chapman Fund
Cowley Charitable Trust
The Foundation for Sport and the Arts
The Foyle Foundation
Francis Finlay Foundation
Genesis Foundation
The Goldsmiths' Company
The Haberdashers' Company
The Paul Hamlyn Foundation
Jerwood Charitable Foundation
John Lyon's Charity
The Magowan Family Foundation
The Mercers' Company
The Diana Parker Charitable Trust
The Laura Pels Foundation
Quercus Charitable Trust
The Eva & Hans K Rausing Trust
The Royal Victoria Hall Foundation
The Peter Jay Sharp Foundation
Skirball Foundation
The Sobell Foundation

The Trusthouse Charitable Foundation
Garfield Weston Foundation
Worshipful Company of Information Technologists

MAJOR SPONSORS
American Airlines
Arts & Business
Barclays
BBC
Bloomberg
Lever Fabergé
Peter Jones

BUSINESS MEMBERS
Aviva plc
Burberry
Lazard
McCann-Erickson
Pemberton Greenish
Redwood
Simons Muirhead & Burton
Slaughter and May

MEDIA MEMBERS
Beatwax
Buena Vista International (UK) Ltd
Columbia Tristar Films (UK)
Hat Trick Productions
Miramax Films
XL Video UK

PRODUCTION SYNDICATE
Anonymous
Jonathan & Sindy Caplan
Kay Hartenstein Saatchi
Richard & Susan Hayden
Peter & Edna Goldstein
Mr & Mrs Jack Keenan
Kadee Robbins
The Viscount & Viscountess Rothermere
William & Hilary Russell

INDIVIDUAL MEMBERS
Patrons
Anonymous
Katie Bradford
Ms Kay Ellen Consolver
Mrs Philip Donald
Celeste Fenichel
Tom & Simone Fenton
Mr & Mrs Jack Keenan
Richard & Robin Landsberger
Duncan Matthews QC

Ian & Carol Sellars
Jan & Michael Topham
Richard Wilson OBE

Benefactors
Martha Allfrey
Anonymous
Jeremy & Amanda Attard-Manché
Lucy Bryn Davies
Danielle Byrne
Yuen-Wei Chew
Robyn Durie
Winstone & Jean Fletcher
Joachim Fleury
Judy & Frank Grace
Homevale Ltd.
Tamara Ingram
Peter & Maria Kellner
Barbara Minto
Nigel Seale
Jenny Sheridan
Peregrine Simon
Brian D Smith
Amanda Vail
Georgia Zaris

Associates
Anastasia Alexander
Anonymous
Eleanor Bowen
Brian Boylan
Mrs Elly Brook JP
Mr & Mrs M Bungey
Ossi & Paul Burger
Mrs Helena Butler
Carole & Neville Conrad
David & Susan Coppard
Margaret Cowper
Barry Cox
Andrew Cryer
Linda & Ronald F. Daitz
David Day
Zoë Dominic
Kim Dunn
Charlotte & Nick Fraser
Jacqueline & Jonathan Gestetner
Michael Goddard
Vivien Goodwin
Sue & Don Guiney
Phil Hobbs - LTRC
Tarek J. Kassem
Carole A. Leng
Lady Lever
Colette & Peter Levy
Mr Watcyn Lewis
Christopher Marcus

David Marks
Nicola McFarland
Mr & Mrs Roderick A McManigal
Eva Monley
Pat Morton
Gavin & Ann Neath
Georgia Oetker
Janet & Michael Orr
Lyndy Payne
Pauline Pinder
William Poeton CBE & Barbara Poeton
Jan & Michael Potter
Jeremy Priestley
John Ritchie
Bernard Shapero
Kathleen Shiach
Lois Sieff OBE
Sue Stapely
Peter & Prilla Stott
Carl & Martha Tack
Will Turner
Anthony Wigram

STAGE HANDS CIRCLE
Graham Billing
Andrew Cryer
Lindy Fletcher
Susan & Richard Hayden
Mr R Hopkins
Philip Hughes Trust
Dr A V Jones
Roger Jospe
Miss A Lind-Smith
Mr J Mills
Nevin Charitable Trust
Janet & Michael Orr
Jeremy Priestley
Ann Scurfield
Brian Smith
Harry Streets
Thai Ping Wong
Richard Wilson OBE
C C Wright

THE AMERICAN FRIENDS OF THE ROYAL COURT THEATRE

AFRCT support the mission of the Royal Court and are primarily focused on raising funds to enable the theatre to produce new work by emerging American writers. Since this not-for-profit organisation was founded in 1997, AFRCT has contributed to ten productions. They have also supported the participation of young artists in the Royal Court's acclaimed International Residency.

If you would like to support the ongoing work of the Royal Court, please contact the Development Department on 020 7565 5050.

ROYAL COURT
JERWOOD THEATRE DOWNSTAIRS

6 - 30 August 2003

The Public Theater, New York production of

TOPDOG/ UNDERDOG

by **Suzan-Lori Parks**
Directed by George C. Wolfe

TOPDOG/UNDERDOG tells the story of two brothers, Lincoln and Booth. Their names, given to them as a joke, foretell a lifetime of sibling rivalry and resentment. Haunted by the past and their obsession with the street con Three Card Monte, the brothers are forced to confront the shattering reality of their future.

Supported by the Laura Pels International Foundation

BOX OFFICE
020 7565 5000
www.royalcourttheatre.com

London Government
Association of
ARTS COUNCIL ENGLAND

FOR THE ROYAL COURT

JERWOOD
NEW PLAYWRIGHTS

Since 1993 Jerwood New Playwrights have contributed to some of the Royal Court's most successful productions, including SHOPPING AND FUCKING by Mark Ravenhill (co-production with Out of Joint), EAST IS EAST by Ayub Khan-Din (co-production with Tamasha), THE BEAUTY QUEEN OF LEENANE by Martin McDonagh (co-production with Druid Theatre Company), THE WEIR by Conor McPherson, REAL CLASSY AFFAIR by Nick Grosso, THE FORCE OF CHANGE by Gary Mitchell, ON RAFTERY'S HILL by Marina Carr (co-production with Druid Theatre Company), 4.48 PSYCHOSIS by Sarah Kane, UNDER THE BLUE SKY by David Eldridge, PRESENCE by David Harrower, HERONS by Simon Stephens, CLUBLAND by Roy Williams, REDUNDANT by Leo Butler, NIGHTINGALE AND CHASE by Zinnie Harris, FUCKING GAMES by Grae Cleugh, BEDBOUND by Enda Walsh, THE PEOPLE ARE FRIENDLY by Michael Wynne, OUTLYING ISLANDS by David Greig and IRON by Rona Munro. This season Jerwood New Playwrights are supporting UNDER THE WHALEBACK by Richard Bean, FLESH WOUND by Ché Walker, FALLOUT by Roy Williams and FOOD CHAIN by Mick Mahoney.

The Jerwood Charitable Foundation is a registered charity dedicated to imaginative and responsible funding and sponsorship of the arts, education, design and other areas of human endeavour and excellence.

HERONS by Simon Stephens
(photo: Pete Jones)

EAST IS EAST by Ayub Khan-Din
(photo: Robert Day)

First published in 2003 by Oberon Books Ltd.
(incorporating Absolute Classics)
521 Caledonian Road, London N7 9RH
Tel: 020 7607 3637 / Fax: 020 7607 3629

e-mail: oberon.books@btinternet.com
www.oberonbooks.com

A catalogue record for this book is available from the British
Library.

ISBN: 1 84002 376 7

Cover photographs: Matthew Mawson

Cover image: Natural

Printed in Great Britain by Antony Rowe Ltd, Chippenham.

Characters

BILLY

JAMIE

CAROL

EMMA

TONY

NAT

for my friend
Pat Brock

Music plays: 'Sing Baby Sing' by The Stylistics.

Lights up.

Enter BILLY – stage right.

At the window he checks his watch before going to the sofa and playing on his Gameboy.

Enter JAMIE – stage right.

He wears a discman and raps along to the music until spotting BILLY.

JAMIE: What you hiding for?

BILLY: Ain't. Told me to wait. They're in the pub across the road.

JAMIE: She shouldn't be in there.

BILLY: Supermarket had a wine promotion, they had a couple of samples.

JAMIE: That's a Paddy's pub.

BILLY: Parking the car she said she had the flavour.

JAMIE: The flavour? Dad won't like that.

BILLY: Is that his local?

JAMIE: No. Oh she asks if you want some crisps bre, you don't.

BILLY: I might, I might not. I'm not your bre either.

JAMIE: I'll put a cap in you if you don't watch yourself.

BILLY: A baseball cap, don't you mean on me?

JAMIE: You don't know nothing, round your way its pure mugs. This is Smith country, you know?

BILLY: Oh and the same postal code makes you a gangster does it?

JAMIE: My play Chilli'd get me a gun here in ten minutes. For true. Now leave my fucking crisps alone.

BILLY: I don't even like them.

JAMIE: Eat enough of them. Tetris! You're crazy blood that's an old persons game. She better not think she's dumping you with me tonight.

BILLY: I'm staying at my Nan's, its Karaoke night at the Labour Club.

JAMIE: Labour Club, Karaoke, you're sad man. While you're tucked up in bed playing with your little winkle. I'll be dancing with all them pop star and actress at Gavin Taylor's party.

BILLY: Never heard of him.

JAMIE: He's the new black kid in Family Affairs, one who's just got out for something he ain't done. Don't you watch the telly? It's Channel Five's flagship soap!

BILLY: Was he in that health warning film about smoking with you?

JAMIE: Boasting you know me in few months. Just landed the lead in a new BBC kids drama. Contracts signed my man, signed!

BILLY: You're, you're the main character?

JAMIE: What's wrong with that? I'm her brother. Know what that means? Means I'm sorted dread. Health warning, been in Grange Hill – for a year. EastEnders, The Bill. Done the lot. What's your highest score?

BILLY: On the A game? Two hundred and nine lines.

JAMIE: Bollocks! That's all you play though ain't it.

BILLY: Play other games.

JAMIE: My mate got a hundred and forty something once. Two hundred and nine's freakish. She shouldn't be in there you know?

BILLY: Isn't she allowed to drink?

JAMIE: Of course she is! We're normal. I need my shirt blad.

BILLY: You've got some make up in your hair.

JAMIE: It's not make up! It's moisturizer – for men.

BILLY: Sounds like make up to me.

JAMIE: Yeah 'cos your a no hoper. I've got to look after me'self. My pal's just been flown out to LA to work with Brad Pitt. I got a recall for that. Who knows next time? Pussy galore out there son. Not a bad way of getting a few quid.

BILLY: You're not how I'd imagine an actor?

JAMIE: No most actors are wankers. I wouldn't do it if it weren't for the gaff around the corner, acting school for street kids.

BILLY: Do all street kids live in houses like this?

JAMIE: What? Either they get a stage school ponce or one of us, to keep it real.

BILLY: You just act yourself?

JAMIE: See! No! (*Jumping about wildly.*) Leave it out mum! Don't go down the pub dad – please! I've had enough of this – I'm leaving! (*Suddenly still.*) But mum you've got to go for your breast cancer check up, it's important and it only takes a few minutes… Don't you think those refugees haves suffered enough guys? (*Jumping about.*) It was him sir! It's not fair! Bag of chips guv'nor yeah?

BILLY: You just have to act like an idiot then?

JAMIE: Just unreal. I always think of it as someone who's never seen a colour telly before.

BILLY: How do you mean?

JAMIE: Say you're playing a kid whose dad's a right boozer – which you are quite a lot of the time. You come home and mum's crying 'cos dad's gone on the piss with the rent money right? Now in real life, most people like that get their rent paid for them by the social but anyway. What the kid would really do is run into his room to see if the old man had flogged his Playstation, but what he does on the telly is put his arm around his old dear and say – don't worry mum, we'll get through it yeah…then cries.

BILLY: I could do that.

JAMIE: You probably have. They want kids with personality.

BILLY: I've got personality.

JAMIE: I'd rather do presenting. My sister does it, or did. Piece of piss. So blood, they've invited a bloke round for your mum, bre's wedged up. Things go well might have yourself a dad.

BILLY: I've got a dad.

JAMIE: The road sweeping drug addict?

BILLY: My dad's two years clean. Plus he's in charge of the road sweepers now.

JAMIE: And you think that's something you can boast about? They're introducing her to Paul Thornton, an award winning director. See all the best people come from the Angel son.

BILLY: Is he a neighbour?

JAMIE: I don't know, he grew up round here, they know him from Youth Club. He got in me dad's cab the other week. I tell you what if he likes the look of your mum, might buy you a new game?

BILLY: Fuck off.

JAMIE: What did you say?

BILLY: You heard.

JAMIE feigns a punch – BILLY flinches.

JAMIE: If it weren't for all this bollocks at school I'd bust you right up, right now.

BILLY: You could try.

JAMIE punches BILLY in the face.

JAMIE: Try – you're only a little mug.

BILLY: I do Tai Kwon Do.

JAMIE: Yeah alright.

BILLY: I do, my uncle trains me. Georgie Brown.

JAMIE: Never heard of him.

BILLY: He was British champion, went to the Olympics!

JAMIE: Wouldn't stop me smashing you all around the gaff.

BILLY: I think it might.

JAMIE: Come on then – I just punched you!

BILLY: I thought you were joking.

JAMIE: You're only being flash cos of this changing room business. I don't know why they're bothering I'm leaving soon. To a nice little CBBC job. You'll be on the dole you.

BILLY: I don't care.

JAMIE: That's why.

BILLY: Where for art thou Romeo.

Enter CAROL and EMMA – stage right laden with supermarket bags.

CAROL: Alright Jame?

JAMIE: Where's me shirt? The Ted Baker.

CAROL: Which one, he's mad about Ted Baker.

EMMA: I can imagine.

CAROL: Which one?

JAMIE: The new one of course.

CAROL: It's been ironed, it's hanging up.

JAMIE: It's not, you knew I'd be wearing that tonight!

CAROL: I'm telling you it's in your wardrobe!

JAMIE: For fucksake!

CAROL: Oi! Less of that you.

JAMIE: Oh yeah Emma does he do Karate?

CAROL: Karate? Chess'd be more up your street wouldn't it Bill?

BILLY: Tell them mum.

EMMA: Every Thursday, diligently.

JAMIE: He reckons the trainer's his uncle.

EMMA: Georgie's not your –

JAMIE: I knew it!

EMMA: He's related to your Nan but he's more like a second cousin or something to you.

JAMIE: He's probably useless anyway.

EMMA: Far from it. He fought for England didn't he?

BILLY: Britain.

JAMIE: Same thing – Hobbit.

BILLY: Of course, how silly of me.

CAROL: It's not quite the same Jame.

BILLY: More or less though Jame.

EMMA: George trained Nat. Billy's father.

BILLY: Go on then, say something?

JAMIE: What? What's he on about?

CAROL: Why don't you two go and play upstairs.

JAMIE: Play?

CAROL: You're always moaning how no one plays on your computer games and that. He's got the new football game Bill.

BILLY: I hate football.

JAMIE: What you wearing that Liverpool badge for then?

BILLY: Ged – my grandfather likes them.

JAMIE: Grandfather, see? He's weird.

CAROL: I tell you what let Bill go on your Playstation and you can go on your dad's X-Box.

EMMA: Tony's got a games console?

CAROL: Don't know why, never uses it.

JAMIE: Saw some trendies playing on one in a film company, came home with one the next day. What about me shirt?

21

CAROL: I said didn't I. I'll find it in a minute! Go on Bill.

JAMIE: Don't go snooping around up there you.

BILLY: I can't try your make up on?

JAMIE: Mum!

CAROL: Moisturizer's not make up Bill. Jamie needs to look after himself love, all celebrities and that do.

JAMIE: Shirt!

CAROL: For fucksake I've only just got through the door!

JAMIE: The newer games and that are in the box on the right.

Exit JAMIE – stage right.

CAROL: Fancy another? Stressful that shopping.

EMMA: Alright, Vodka and Orange.

Exit CAROL – stage left.

BILLY: I'd love him to come to training.

EMMA: What's all this about Georgie being your uncle.

BILLY: I wish he was.

EMMA: Why?

BILLY: He, I feel safe with Georgie.

EMMA: What about your dad?

BILLY: He's a bit intense now isn't he.

EMMA: I wouldn't know.

BILLY: His letters are intense.

EMMA: He writes every week when I was at school I was lucky to –

BILLY: Why don't I just go round Nan's now?

EMMA: One a term. Tony's going to take you.

BILLY: Mum, why don't we just go on holiday with Grannie and Ged?

EMMA: Because after three weeks with my mother and her husband I'll be – (*Mimes injecting her arm.*) Then you'd be getting two intense letters a week.

Enter CAROL – stage left. From a tray she hands EMMA a drink and BILLY a packet of crisps.

CAROL: I'll just get his shirt out the way and I can relax.

Exit CAROL – stage right.

BILLY: The bus goes straight from up the road.

EMMA: Tony's taking you in his cab. It'll be dark soon.

BILLY: I come back from Nan's all the time in the dark. Later than –

EMMA: You're nagging Billy. Please.

BILLY: You just want me out of the way.

EMMA: Can you blame me?

BILLY: Come on mum, you loved it last time, the old Karaoke.

EMMA: I can't Carol's cooking a meal.

BILLY: Her food never tastes of anything. You have to put loads of salt –

EMMA: No.

BILLY: My dad's coming up.

EMMA: When?

BILLY: Soon. I phoned him, yesterday.

23

EMMA: I don't know if that's a very good idea. Tony says –

BILLY: What could Tony possibly know about my dad?

EMMA: He knows those people your father owes money. They're from around here.

BILLY: Dad's paid them.

EMMA: Not according to what Tony's heard.

BILLY: He's paid for the drugs he took, he's just not paying for what anyone else has taken.

EMMA: It's no wonder you find his letters intense if this is the sort of thing he writes about.

BILLY: He told me. When I was down at Easter.

EMMA: Well Tony knows a lot of people and –

BILLY: Really? We're round here all the time and I haven't seen any one.

EMMA: You're fourteen you don't know what you're talking about. Anyway, I'll be seeing one of them tonight.

Enter CAROL – stage right.

BILLY: Oh of course, The Maestro.

CAROL: Who's that?

BILLY: Orson Welles.

EMMA: It's nothing Carol. He's just sulking about tonight.

CAROL: Got to let your mum have a life of her own Bill.

EMMA: Quite.

BILLY: Georgie'll be down there.

EMMA: And? Oh don't be ridiculous.

CAROL: Aye? Aye?

EMMA: Billy?

BILLY: She kissed him, snogged him!

EMMA: I was drunk. God Carol are you short of Orange Juice?

CAROL: When was this then?

BILLY: A few weeks ago!

EMMA: It was nothing.

BILLY: Nothing?

CAROL: He's close to tears Em?

BILLY: She could have snogged anyone! Georgie's mine! Mine and dad's.

EMMA: I've said I was sorry.

BILLY: Oh so that makes it alright? So every time you get drunk and make a fool of yourself, that's what I get – sorry?

EMMA: Every time? Could you be any more melodramatic?

BILLY: Could you be any more bizarre? This whole phase, the bakery and –

EMMA: Shut up! Shut up! You precocious little – Tai Kwon Do? I don't think so. What do they call you the Weedy Warrior?

BILLY: You don't need big muscles!

EMMA: Or, The Bed Wetter?

CAROL: Emma!

EMMA: Get bloody Georgie to wash your pissy sheets for you.

BILLY: I've stopped, you, you trollop! You slag!

CAROL: Billy!

BILLY: Fuck off! Just fuck off!

EMMA grabs BILLY by the scruff of the neck and begins shaking him – violently.

CAROL: Emma don't. You're, you'll break his neck!

EMMA: Happy now – fucker! Little fucker!

BILLY: Go on then kill me!

CAROL: (*Pulling EMMA off.*) That's enough!

EMMA releases her grip and backs away.

BILLY: That was intelligent.

EMMA: I need a cigarette now, is that what you want?

BILLY: No.

EMMA: It feels like it. Have you got something to say, to Carol?

BILLY: Yeah, I'm sorry Carol.

CAROL: Alright.

BILLY produces his Gameboy and begins playing on it.

EMMA: God they're handy those things. Drawback's the batteries.

CAROL: Is that it, back to normal?

EMMA: There's no point sustaining it, delving into it.

CAROL: I wouldn't let my kids speak to me like that. He ought to see someone, he's unbalanced.

EMMA: He probably is but then again we all have our little quirks.

CAROL: I don't know, that bed wetting's not a good sign.

EMMA: He hasn't done it for, it must be a year now.

BILLY: Over a year actually.

CAROL: That's shaken me up. You alright Bill?

EMMA: Carol? I'd know if he wasn't. Billy look I'm sorry I shouldn't have said that, about the Karate. I love you.

BILLY: I love you.

CAROL: Right, you want a drink?

EMMA: Hadn't we better get started with the cooking?

CAROL: Won't take long. Bill why don't you go upstairs and play. Your mum needs to get changed and that for tonight.

EMMA: Now, oughtn't I have a shower first?

Enter JAMIE – stage right.

JAMIE: Where's dad I need some money for tonight.

CAROL: How much?

JAMIE: I don't know, fifty quid.

CAROL: It's a party!

JAMIE: I've got to take a bottle, Champagne ain't cheap mum.

CAROL: They've got it in the offie on Upper Street.

JAMIE: You expect me to take something out of the bargain bin? Fuck it I won't bother going then.

CAROL: You've got to go!

JAMIE: Bollocks do I.

CAROL: Champagne's not fifty quid a pop!

JAMIE: Good ones are ain't they Emma.

CAROL: Couldn't you just –

JAMIE: I'm not going if I haven't got any money.

CAROL: Let me see what I've got. Thing is Emma it's important 'cos they get to know you. That's how you got EastEnders wasn't it Jame. I've got thirty, get the rest off your dad but don't say I've given –

JAMIE: (*Snatching cash.*) I'm not fucking stupid.

Exit JAMIE – stage right.

CAROL: Come back here you!

JAMIE: (*Offstage.*) Bollocks!

CAROL: It's different with him, more cheeky. These telly bods love it.

BILLY: He's so charismatic.

CAROL: They know what they're doing Bill. Anyway get upstairs so your mum can start getting ready.

EMMA: There's plenty of time yet.

CAROL: You don't want to be panicking at the last minute. I've got those shoes for you.

EMMA: Where are they? Is there a mirror in the bathroom?

CAROL: Do it down here, they're just in the hall. Have a shower after when you know what you're wearing. Tony won't be barging in he's probably picked up a fair, can't blame him – from the airport.

EMMA: I forgot he was taking Alice. Is he still dropping Billy at his Nan's?

CAROL: Yeah. I dread to think what she's going to be getting up to out there. Mind you she's young free and single ain't she.

EMMA: Where's she going?

CAROL: Emma – Aia Napa! Come on, let's get your outfit sorted.

EMMA: Oh alright.

EMMA begins to unbutton her top.

CAROL: Hang about, Bill have a go on Jamie's Playstation while your mum's getting changed eh?

EMMA: Seen it all before haven't you Billy.

CAROL: Yeah but he's getting older now Emma, it's what's it isn't it – inappropriate.

EMMA: Oh is it?

CAROL: Go on Bill, Jamie's in our room on the X-Box.

BILLY: I'd rather play on that.

CAROL: Well you can't.

Exit BILLY – stage right.

EMMA: I shouldn't have done that, you know with George but we were all having such a nice time.

CAROL: This Karate trainer, how old is he then?

EMMA: I don't know, must be in his mid-fifties. He's handsome.

CAROL: Straight. What you just kissed him in front of everyone?

EMMA: Yeah, how long is Alice out there?

CAROL: Supposed to be a fortnight but I wouldn't be surprised if it's longer. You know she gets a grand a pop for a Personal Appearance? Imagine she'll be doing a few out there.

EMMA: So, she's stopped doing The Pop Files?

CAROL: Some of the other presenters were getting on her nerves. She'd done it for over a year anyway. See that picture of her in The Sun the other day? They love her they do. Tony's been working with her on a few ideas for stuff.

EMMA: For breakfast TV?

CAROL: She's had enough of that. Starting at half-five in the morning, barbaric ain't it. She'd be going straight from a club to work, not right.

EMMA: Come on Carol she shouldn't be out in clubs then.

CAROL: She had to be out to know what was going on and that didn't she. Anyway she gets more in half an hour doing a PA than she does in a week doing the show.

EMMA: Surely it's the exposure from the show that generates the PAs?

CAROL: Emma if you read the papers and that, she's in them. She had a meeting with the BBC today. They only expected her to cancel her holiday for it.

EMMA: They scheduled knowing she'd be away?

CAROL: No! It was booked months ago, she forgot. Think they're God's gift that lot, terrible payers and all.

EMMA: They can't be that bad?

CAROL: No not compared to you down the bakery and that obviously. How you getting on down there?

EMMA: I like it. Tina's fun.

CAROL: You don't think we look alike do you?

EMMA: I don't know, you are sisters. Her voice is similar.

CAROL: Oh God don't, got a voice like a fog horn Tina. She's treating you alright, she can be a bit bossy and that?

EMMA: I've always found something reassuring about bakeries. I suppose its the smell. At school we used to be allowed down to the –

CAROL: Let's get you done before he comes back. I'll get the shoes.

EMMA: Actually I've bought a pair with me.

The phone rings. CAROL answers it.

CAROL: Just talking about you… Oh yeah? It's Tina, she reckons if he's no value tonight, should meet them down The Crown.

EMMA: I might.

CAROL: Says she might. Oi! Teen how much you paying her? She just done two hundred and fifty quid on a dress!

Exit CAROL stage left.

EMMA begins unbuttoning her top.

EMMA: Where's that dress?

Enter CAROL – stage left carrying a pair of high heel shoes and a bottle of vodka.

CAROL: They're nice, just gone bit tight.

CAROL fills their glasses and stands by the window.

EMMA: Oh, Marks and Sparks?

CAROL: Designer range. Let's have a look then.

EMMA: I couldn't see the dress.

CAROL: It's here somewhere. I was surprised it went through on your card, two-fifty?

EMMA: Oh it's fine as long as you pay them on time.

EMMA takes off her top as CAROL searches the bags for the dress.

CAROL: Here it is.

EMMA: I've got another bra, to push them up a bit.

CAROL: They look alright in that. It was just as good that dress for eighty quid?

EMMA slips off her jeans.

EMMA: No it wasn't. Matching knickers for later. You never know.

CAROL: Got nice legs ain't you. So firm!

EMMA: Something to be said for having to walk everywhere. Carol these heels are outrageous.

CAROL: They make your legs look about four foot long.

EMMA studies herself in the mirror.

EMMA: I look like such a tart!

EMMA performs a lewd dance movement.

CAROL: How do you do that in those?

EMMA: What, this?

CAROL: Fuck me that's horny.

EMMA: It's pretty hackneyed Carol. Listen, you think it's wrong, bringing that underwear – slutty?

CAROL: How do you mean? There's no point being coy about it. You're both adults. Have you ever done Pole Dancing or that then?

EMMA: Carol!

CAROL: Well?

EMMA: I've danced in clubs, as I don't know, a Go-Go dancer I suppose you'd call it. But not as a stripper or anything.

CAROL: Had a lot of experiences and that haven't you.

EMMA: Not lately. I've got doubts about tonight as well to be honest. I mean he's still married.

CAROL: Separated.

EMMA: It's not divorced. I don't even know if I'm up for it.

CAROL: You don't want to end up a single mum on the social love. You ever been out with Tina and them when they go and watch these fellas stripping and that?

EMMA: No. I've heard it can get a little raucous.

CAROL: I can't believe some of the stuff she tells me.

EMMA: I can't believe these heels. I think they're a bit much.

CAROL: Look mental. Think it's bad me not having much experience?

EMMA: Why do you?

EMMA puts on her new dress.

CAROL: Tina's had a few experiences.

EMMA: Perhaps she just enjoys it more.

CAROL: You think I'm what's it? I'm not. I enjoy it alright.

EMMA: Good for you. I'll wear my own shoes actually.

CAROL: I can't dance like that, I tried it once and he howled up.

EMMA: You must have felt awful?

CAROL: Married life ain't it.

33

EMMA: I don't think humiliation's a prerequisite Carol.

CAROL: Not married are you.

EMMA: I'd rather not be if that's what's entailed.

CAROL: Probably was funny…I don't know if I was that bad though.

EMMA: I'll tell you.

CAROL: How do you mean?

EMMA: I'll watch you dance and tell you what I think.

CAROL: Leave it out.

EMMA: It's easy look.

CAROL: Yeah it's easy for you. I'm too fat.

EMMA: You've got to have something to shake.

CAROL: I'm just no good at it.

EMMA: Come on Carol.

CAROL: Jamie's upstairs.

EMMA: Oh right. We'd better get on with the cooking then.

CAROL: Hang about. I don't want one of them coming down.

CAROL closes the door.

EMMA: What about music?

CAROL: I won't be able to hear will I.

CAROL begins to dance.

EMMA: Whoa! Take your top off.

CAROL: I couldn't.

EMMA: Mine was off.

CAROL downs her drink.

CAROL: I can't believe I'm doing this.

EMMA: Get your tits out.

CAROL: Emma?

CAROL looks out of the window before unzipping her top.

EMMA: Big aren't they. Don't cover them up!

CAROL: You don't think they're undignified? That's what he reckons.

EMMA: Most blokes love big tits?

CAROL: What about you?

EMMA: I think they're fascinating. You can't really move properly in that skirt though can you?

CAROL: I can't take it off! He'll be back in a minute I know he will.

EMMA: Alright just pull it up then. Nice and nasty.

CAROL: Don't.

EMMA: Oh for God sake, hike it up will you?

CAROL: Jamie's upstairs.

EMMA: Oh sod Jamie.

As CAROL begins to pull up her skirt there's a noise off.

CAROL: That's him! Bastard spoils everything.

TONY: (*Off.*) Carol!

CAROL smooths down her skirt and zips up her top.

CAROL: In here!

TONY enters – stage right – carrying a boxed Playstation 2.

TONY: Alright. What?

CAROL: You said you were coming straight back to take Bill round his Nan's?

TONY: Dropped some Northerners at Euston, earns sixty quid. Love a bit of Reebok that mob.

CAROL: She's been waiting!

EMMA: Carol it's fine.

TONY: You ain't started cooking yet?

CAROL: It's too late now.

TONY: What?

CAROL: I thought we could get take away.

TONY: You've just spunked a hundred quid on this lot!

CAROL: We can eat it in the week. It's not a hundred quid anyway.

TONY: I bet there's over seventy quid's worth in those bags that's meant to be for tonight. You want to get it out and add it up Carol?

CAROL: There's not a hundred quid's worth. I thought we could try that new Thai place on St John's Street, supposed to be mental.

TONY: Leave it out. You ain't even tried it and you want to serve it up?

CAROL: Emma ain't that gaff alright?

EMMA: From what I've read it's –

TONY: What about this lot?

CAROL: I just said, we can eat it in the week. He's supposed to be here in half an hour.

TONY: I don't know. You two been boozing?

CAROL: Boozing? You should get in that shower.

EMMA: Am I going to have time for one?

CAROL: He don't take long.

TONY: Yeah but I'm thorough!

CAROL: I didn't say you weren't.

TONY: The implication was there.

CAROL: Can't say anything can I.

TONY: Take away? What's he going to think Paul Thornton, being invited around for a load of shit from the Bengal Lancer? He's an award winning director Carol.

CAROL: Thai we're getting! It's different. The way you've been banging on about him's made me nervous.

TONY: All I've said is he's done well for himself.

CAROL: Said a bit more than that ain't he Emma.

TONY: Only to show he's worth her while.

CAROL: Well she's made an effort, what do you reckon.

TONY: Yeah. I don't know about this Thai, at least we've eaten from the Lancer, know it's decent.

CAROL: It was in The Standard's top ten Indians.

TONY: Bit Wolverhampton. There nothing else?

EMMA: I'll make the food.

CAROL: Don't be daft. What about that Tapas bar on Chap?

TONY: Chapel Street? I tell you what, I'll pop into Manzie's for some Pie & Mash! If there's a stall still open I'll get some Cockles & Whelks for starters?

CAROL: That Tapas bar's blinding, Emma said!

TONY: Is it?

EMMA: I liked it.

TONY: We'll get some Thai, still half trendy ain't it.

CAROL: We've never had it have we.

TONY: I've had it from Soho Thai. Best in London.

CAROL: When?

TONY: Me and Kenny had it the other week.

CAROL: First I've heard about it.

TONY: I don't tell you everything.

CAROL: Feels like it.

TONY: Where's he soppy bollocks?

CAROL: Upstairs on your game thing. Billy's on his.

TONY: Oh yeah here are. Got it off Kenny. Brand new.

EMMA: Oh but –

TONY: Don't worry about it. Time he had one of his own.
Don't get me wrong he's always welcome around here
and that but not the same as having his own is it.

CAROL: How much was that?

TONY: He couldn't get into it Kenny.

CAROL: How much?

TONY: One and a half alright?

CAROL: Not really no.

EMMA: The thing is Tony –

TONY: It's chipped so it plays all the pirate games, DVDs.
Got a shipment. For a multi-million pound outfit they do
like a bit of small time.

CAROL: All money. You don't look too pleased Emma.

EMMA: He hates Playstation Tony. I told you that.

TONY: That's just 'cos he ain't got one.

EMMA: I've offered to get it for him.

TONY: I'm not being funny Emma but he don't want you
    spending on one of these when he knows how skint you
    are and that.

EMMA: I'm not that skint.

CAROL: You will be now. Two-fifty she paid for that.

TONY: Straight? No listen, he'll love it honestly.

CAROL: Can't we give him it for Christmas? When's his
    birthday?

EMMA: A couple of months ago.

TONY: Let's just give it to him now. What's wrong with
    you?

CAROL: It's a lot of money just to – don't want him
    thinking they grow on trees do we Emma.

TONY: Want to save some money? Cook some of that.

CAROL: I'm just saying!

TONY: It's the least we can do.

CAROL: Emma's happy with the arrangement as it stands.
    She's looking forward to that holiday.

EMMA: This isn't meant to be instead is it? I'd rather the
    holiday, so would Billy.

TONY: I'm not so sure about that.

EMMA: I am. He has very strong feelings about the Sony
    Playstation.

TONY: It's not instead of anyway. It's as well as. I just thought it'd be nice – honestly.

EMMA: Right. Am I going to have time to shower?

TONY: You go first seeing as, you know.

EMMA: I can relax once it's out of the way.

CAROL: Use any of the towels up there. I'll get him out of our room, you can change in there.

EMMA: I won't be long. Though I will be thorough.

EMMA picks up her stuff and exits – stage right.

TONY: Spoke to him earlier, Paul Thornton. Thinks he's going to fuck it.

CAROL: Probably will. She wants it.

TONY: What she said that?

CAROL: No but she's brought all nice underwear with her and that.

TONY: I told you, she's hanging out for it.

CAROL: She's entitled to be, ain't had it for a couple of years!

TONY: I wonder if she thingy, you know?

CAROL: Has a fiddle? I'd imagine so.

TONY: Mind you she might not go for him. He's a bit full of himself. Put on some weight an' all. You think we're doing the right thing?

EMMA: It was your idea.

TONY: I know but – where's she get changed then?

CAROL: Paul say anything about Jamie doing that advert?

TONY: He looked him up in Spotlight and – you think Jamie needs new photos?

CAROL: No. Why?

TONY: Paul, he reckons he's looking for someone a bit, a bit better looking.

CAROL: Better looking, better looking? Cheeky bastard. What did you say? He should talk to all them tarts at school who want Jamie up them. Better looking, liberty.

TONY: That photographer said didn't he – Jamie was a bit taller he could be a model. I'm sure he's a better judge than Paul Thornton.

CAROL: Paul fucking Thornton. He's no Ginola his'self. What about Alice, for the daughter?

TONY: Her being a presenter's the problem there. Anyway we've got a few ideas, vehicles sorted now.

CAROL: Imagine how much those actors got out of the Oxo family?

TONY: One who played the mum's a household name now.

CAROL: Alice ain't worked for a while you know?

TONY: Only left the show a few weeks ago. What?

CAROL: It's nearly four months Tone. You sure about that Playst–

TONY: It's a sweetener. I'm going to talk to her about buying that flat off the council. She can move in with Bill's Nan and we'll rent –

CAROL: Emma's not going to go and live with her ex's mum Tone.

TONY: I think she might if I offer her six grand, that's a lot of money to someone like her. Plus it'd stop the kid being so weird having his Nan about, be company for the old dear and all.

CAROL: You're just going to embarrass everyone.

TONY: Don't know about this Rolex.

CAROL: Ain't stopped again?

TONY: Think it's a bit big on me? It's alright on Kenny.

CAROL: You nagged for over a year about that.

TONY: I think it's too big.

CAROL: You could tighten the strap but that's how they wear them, loose like that.

TONY: How cab drivers and spivs wear them.

CAROL: Oh shit. How do you mean?

TONY: Fair at Hambros Bank the other day's reached for his change and his cuff's ridden up – got the exact same model.

CAROL: That's alright, he ain't a low lifer.

TONY: It was over his wrist bone – hidden.

CAROL: So tighten it.

TONY: But then no one would – it's a diver's watch the only diving this does is into me change bag.

CAROL: You getting fed up with work Tone?

TONY pulls the watch up over his wrist bone.

TONY: How does this look?

CAROL: Can't see any difference. I don't like the watch anyway.

TONY: Could have said when I was laying out seventeen hundred quid!

CAROL: I did.

TONY: Does it make me look like a cabbie?

CAROL: Thought that was what you wanted.

TONY: It was.

CAROL: Jesus, you've only been at it a few years!

TONY: Four.

CAROL: Took five to do The Knowledge.

TONY: It's, it's doing my brain in – honestly.

CAROL: What – the traffic?

TONY: Part of the job. No, it's listening to those loud ignorant bastards everyday.

CAROL: Punters are part of the job Tone.

TONY: Punters? I'm talking about the other cabbies.

CAROL: We've just had a twenty grand refurb on Canonbury!

TONY: Yeah, yeah and look at the rent its pulling in now!

CAROL: I'm not saying…how're we going to pay it off if you're not out in the cab? My wages won't cover –

TONY: The milk bill. I'm not going to just stop.

CAROL: You've done it before. My money's not that bad for part time.

TONY: I'll sort something out, you know that. It's just I thought they were all like Kenny and that lot from the cafe. To be fair though, they ain't all I'd imagined. I didn't realize there were so many muggy ones.

CAROL: Cabbies? There's a lot of them Tony, bound to be a few divs.

TONY: Other day in the cafe, Kenny's described himself as – a ponce in a mobile begging bowl – everyone's laughed.

CAROL: It's funny.

TONY: I can't get the image out of my mind, feel like one of those Pakis who's had his legs twisted at birth.

CAROL: Talking of spastics, you love it when you all take them kids down to the Seaside!

TONY: Yeah that's one day a year, rest of the time we're cutting each other's throats over a fiver fare.

CAROL: Pink cloud's over that's all.

TONY: I've stopped going to the cafe.

CAROL: Yeah I thought you'd been earning more.

TONY: In there last week and fellow – just past out – starts taking the piss out of me shoes. Postman, delivering letters a month ago, taking the piss out of me? Thought I'd left all that behind with the plastering.

CAROL: That didn't last long.

TONY: Once we've paid off Canonbury I'm starting a chauffeuring business, still use the Knowledge that way.

CAROL: Not a lot of difference from cabbing is there?

TONY: Difference being, after a while I can take on more drivers and build the company up. If the kids do alright, might be able to use their contacts to ferry celebrities about.

CAROL: Has Paul called? He's not going to show. Fuck him anyway if Jamie's not getting that advert.

TONY: Might be a ploy see if that's all we're after.

CAROL: It is.

TONY: This won't be the only ad campaign he's going to do.

CAROL: He's not going to show anyway.

TONY: For fucksake he phoned last night to confirm it!

CAROL: Give him a ring, make sure.

TONY: What save you cooking? She got changed down here, where were you then?

CAROL: Sorting out Jamie's shirt for tonight.

TONY: What's the figure like on it?

CAROL: It's alright.

TONY: See the way she was posing when you told me to look at her dress? That ponce Thornton's going to get the benefit.

CAROL: Benefit?

TONY: You know what I mean. Don't it bother you, the way she acts around me?

CAROL: No…it's quite sweet in a way.

TONY: I wouldn't like to be left alone with her for long.

CAROL: You wouldn't trust her, or yourself?

TONY: Slow down! Dread to think where it's been. I'll give Paul a bell eh?

TONY produces an address book.

CAROL: Tell him we're running a few minutes late.

TONY: Message – Paul it's Tony, we're running a tad late but it's alright. Give me a ring let me know what's what.

CAROL: What's what?

TONY: He might be on a shoot or something.

CAROL: You should've asked if he likes Thai.

TONY: Hit him with the take away aspect when he gets here. What about this kettle? I could wear it over the wrist, with a T-shirt?

CAROL: I don't know. Funny Paul getting into your cab eh?

TONY: Get better people than him all the time with radio jobs.

CAROL: He was never out of that table tennis room.

TONY: That was his domain, him and that weird little black kid who always had fluff in his hair.

CAROL: I can't see how he made it really. He didn't seem to have any personality.

TONY: Directors don't. Is that her finishing up there?

CAROL: Better get Jamie out of our room so she can get ready.

TONY: Lot of people used to ignore Paul. I didn't.

CAROL: You never knocked about with him though.

TONY: I know but I was alright to him.

CAROL: Wonder how he got into it. Done well though ain't he, to be award winning.

TONY: Only for adverts. He's not Martin Scorsese.

CAROL: Separated though? Shame. Don't say anything about buying her flat Tone.

TONY: Dozy bitch ain't going to buy it. That's a property going to waste! Six grand'd be like the pools to her.

CAROL: I don't think she's not that dozy.

TONY: I do. Listen, you'd still be living on the Packington if it weren't for me.

CAROL: Oh don't start.

TONY: Asked about you Paul. Nice of him to remember you and that wasn't it.

CAROL: Why wouldn't he remember me?

TONY: Fuck me don't go into one. I'm just saying.

CAROL: Nice of him to remember you wasn't it.

Enter JAMIE – stage right.

JAMIE: She's out the shower. Dad –

CAROL: Tone jump in there sharpish, you've got to drop
    Bill off and pick up the Thai.

TONY: Can't you do that? I'm driving all day!

CAROL: When am I going to get ready?

TONY: What difference? It's her he's going to be ogling.

CAROL: On my life you're brain damage you.

JAMIE: Before you kick off, I need an apple.

TONY: Have a look in these bags.

JAMIE: I need a score dad.

TONY: How do I know you're not using it – to score?

JAMIE: What?

TONY: How do I know this ain't going on Es and Charlie?

JAMIE: Mum!

CAROL: That was Donovan. He's stopped hanging around
    with him!

TONY: You don't need money for a party – that's why
    people like them.

JAMIE: I've been through all this with her!

CAROL: What if they go out for something to eat, or onto
    a club?

TONY: What club's he going to – he's sixteen!

JAMIE: Fuck it. I won't go then.

TONY: Don't.

CAROL: It's for his career!

TONY: He's starting that series in a couple of months!

CAROL: There's going to be all sorts there ain't there Jame.

JAMIE: Producers, casting directors everything.

TONY: For some kid's eighteenth?

JAMIE: His mum runs Channel 4 drama.

TONY: They've got a black woman running it? No wonder it's –

JAMIE: She's the head geezer's assistant but she half runs it.

CAROL: Alright?

TONY hands JAMIE the cash.

JAMIE: Get the idiot out of my room will you.

Exit JAMIE – stage right.

CAROL: Can't keep treating him like a criminal over one mistake.

TONY: He got caught the once. How do we know he's not getting out of his head every time he goes out? Speaking of which, I saw that fellow. Top notch gear.

CAROL: You've had some?

TONY: No. He said. I hid it in the cab. Under the –

CAROL: How much did you get?

TONY: Half a gram. What we get at Christmas.

CAROL: Not going to last long between four of us. He probably has it all the time. I bet she'd do that in one line.

TONY: Nothing clever about that Carol. I only got it in case, you know, so we didn't look square.

CAROL: I don't know why you bothered. Half a gram. Look like right wankers.

TONY: We'll say it's all we got left, that our guy's run out.

Enter EMMA – stage right wearing her new dress and her high heels.

EMMA: Hi.

CAROL: What shoes are they then?

EMMA: L K Bennett.

CAROL: Sale?

EMMA: I'm not sure. I've had them a while.

TONY: She's got some from there. Got them years ago.

CAROL: No I haven't.

TONY: Yes you have!

CAROL: I ain't Tone. I should know what shoe's I've got!

TONY: Obviously don't do you! Those red ones with the metal heel.

CAROL: They're Johnny Moke Tone.

TONY: Johnny Moke? Even better then ain't they Johnny Moke!

EMMA: Heavens Tony, you're passionate about women's shoes.

CAROL: He can get like this about anything.

TONY: I was going to get you some from L K Bennett the other Christmas. Remember – honestly.

CAROL: You taking Bill now or after your shower?

TONY: Sure you didn't have a pair from there, years ago?

CAROL: Fucking positive. Nice aren't they.

TONY: Alright. Bill! Oi! Bill! Got something for you down here mate!

CAROL: Save having to talk to his Nan.

EMMA: They get on very well actually.

TONY: Interesting. Think they could live together?

EMMA: Why?

TONY: You put in to buy your place – move in with his Nan and when the three years are up you sell to me and I give you fifteen grand.

EMMA: That property's worth considerably more than fifteen grand.

TONY: Yeah but you'd have to spend a lot on it, just to get to mortgageable standard – honestly. Depending on what I can rent it at, might be able to bung you a few bob every month and all. I tell you what, I'll throw in six grand now, to cover your expenses and what not? You said her place is too big for her. You'd have a room of your own – each, live in-sitter for Bill. Be company for the old dear and all.

EMMA: I don't think so.

CAROL: I told you. I fucking told you! You're embarrassing me!

TONY: Embarrass? I'm trying to help her out!

CAROL: Just get in the shower eh?

TONY: Emma I don't need to – I could get a million for this tomorrow. What four beds are coming to around here – honestly!

Enter BILLY – stage right.

EMMA: Are you all set, to go?

TONY: I've got something for you.

CAROL: Close your eyes!

BILLY: Do I have to?

TONY: Course not! Here are.

TONY hands over the Playstation 2.

BILLY: Thanks but –

TONY: Comes with a loads of games – good 'uns. It's
    chipped and that so it does everything bar wank you off.
    Sorry girls.

BILLY: That's great.

CAROL: Don't sound like it?

BILLY: Mum?

TONY: I thought you'd love it Bill?

EMMA: He's very loyal to Sega. His dad got him a…?

BILLY: Saturn. What's so funny?

TONY: What a pile of pony that was!

BILLY: No they weren't!

EMMA: He had a lot of hope in the Dreamcast –

TONY: It's obsolete!

BILLY: That doesn't make it a bad games consul. Sony just
    brainwash everyone with advertising. The Playstation's
    just for part time gamers. It's crap.

CAROL: You spend enough time on that one up there.

TONY: You don't want it?

BILLY: No. Thank you. Can I go to Nan's now. I think she might have gone down the club by now.

TONY: You think those Nips are running around Tokyo talking about how loyal Bill is? Going to give you shares in Sega are they?

BILLY: I just don't like Playstation that's all.

TONY: Grow up will you for fucksake.

EMMA: Tony, you're frightening him.

TONY: I'm not am I Bill?

BILLY: No.

EMMA: Well you're frightening me. It's only a computer game.

TONY: Yeah, it is and it isn't. I tell you what Bill, make your life a lot easier when you want to swap games mate?

BILLY: I'm fine as I am.

TONY's mobile phone rings.

TONY: Alright Paul!

CAROL: We're not ready yet!

TONY: Yeah turn right at the Police station and we're just down the road, more or less opposite the boozer…Yeah that's it. See you in a minute.

CAROL: A minute?

TONY: He's on Pentonville Road. Better get that food ordered.

CAROL: We're not ready!

TONY: I should have told him to stop off at the Thai gaff and bring the fucking food eh?

CAROL: Why not, he's not helping Jamie out. Fuck him.

TONY: What about Emma?

CAROL: Oh yeah. I suppose so.

TONY: Bill take this, you don't like it, sell it.

BILLY: Can I?

TONY: Course! But you've got to give it a chance. How's that?

BILLY and TONY shake hands.

Exit BILLY – with console.

CAROL: Are you mad. You've just spent –

TONY: Will you shut up! I'm trying to help the kid out!

EMMA: It's a shame in a way. He's held out for so long.

CAROL: He might not like it.

TONY: He'll love it.

CAROL: Jamie could have it if he don't –

TONY: Jamie's got one.

CAROL: Paul can drive Bill round while we're getting sorted.

TONY: Are you mad?

EMMA: Does he know I've got a fourteen year old?

CAROL: Yeah. I suppose so?

TONY: He knows what to expect.

EMMA: Oh, and what's that then Tony?

TONY: That you've got a kid and that.

CAROL: Shall I go first, in the shower?

EMMA: She's got a kid's not too enticing?

CAROL: Stop fishing. He's not going to say you're a dragon is he!

TONY: Obviously. Order that Thai. I'm having a quick shower.

Exit TONY – stage right.

CAROL: Take my car and drop Bill will you.

EMMA: I can't. You know I'm banned Carol.

CAROL: I haven't got time to argue Emma. Here's the keys… We're doing this for you. You could help out love.

EMMA: You think it'll be alright?

Enter BILLY – stage right holding Playstation.

CAROL: Your mum's driving you. I've got to get this lot in the fridge. Emma, you'll be fine.

BILLY: She's banned. We'll get a cab mum.

Enter JAMIE – stage right wearing a fresh shirt.

JAMIE: Can I have a sandwich?

CAROL: Help me get this lot put away first.

Exit CAROL and JAMIE – stage left carrying the shopping.

EMMA: I don't know if I've got enough for a cab.

BILLY: Nan'll give you some cash.

CAROL: (*Off.*) In a minute! Get out of the way. Wait in there!

Enter JAMIE – stage left.

JAMIE: And don't forget the crisps!

EMMA: Carol, I'll be as quick as I can!

CAROL: (*Off.*) You still here? Hurry up Emma!

BILLY: Come on mum.

CAROL: (*Off.*) You want salad cream on this Jame?

Exit EMMA and BILLY – stage right.

JAMIE: Just how you do it. I don't know do I!

CAROL: (*Off.*) You're fucking useless that's why!

JAMIE presses a number into his mobile phone and speaks quietly into it.

JAMIE: Chilli blad I got the other fifty so I can take the ten at the price we said… Me, Jamie!… No I get confused with the powder… That one across the street from me? No one goes in there bre… Oh yeah of course… Five minutes, laters.

Enter CAROL – stage left. She hands JAMIE a plate containing a sandwich – surrounded by crisps.

CAROL: Who's that? Got to be someone?

JAMIE: Stevie. Does the tube go straight to Hampstead?

CAROL: Yeah, or you change at Camden Town. Stevie from Fools & Horses? So funny ain't it. Oh I've got to order that Thai! Do that for me Jame while I get daddy out the shower. Please?

JAMIE: Alright, alright. Where's the number?

CAROL: There's a flyer in the desk. Hurry up!

Exit CAROL – stage right. Searching the draw JAMIE finds a wad of cash and pockets a twenty pound note before discovering the flyer.

JAMIE: What do you want – to eat?

CAROL: (*Off.*) Get them to sort it out, meal for four people!

JAMIE: Is that the Thai gaff?… You sound Chinese… Yeah a meal for four people… Oh, hang on – they've got two different ones for four!

The door bell sounds – off.

CAROL: (*Off.*) Get that will you!

JAMIE: I'm not sure. Which one gives you the most?

The door bell goes again.

CAROL: (*Off.*) Jame!

JAMIE: I'm talking to the Thai people!

TONY: (*Off.*) Stop and answer the fucking door!

JAMIE: You're doing my brain in!

JAMIE slams down the phone.

CAROL: (*Off.*) Jamie!

A half dressed TONY appears – stage left.

TONY: Get the door fuckwit.

JAMIE exits – stage left.

TONY enters – left right. TONY frantically tidies up.

Enter JAMIE – stage right.

Exit TONY – stage left.

Enter NAT – stage right.

JAMIE: Be down in a minute. Want a drink?

NAT: I'm fine thanks.

JAMIE: What are you working on?

NAT: Working on?

JAMIE: Yeah, at the minute.

NAT: At the minute, Fear of Intimacy.

JAMIE: Oh, is that a series?

NAT: Series of disasters.

JAMIE: I've got one coming up, series. For the Beeb.

NAT: That's nice.

Enter TONY – stage right.

TONY: Who are you?

NAT: I come for my boy.

TONY: Oh right. Emma's taken him round your mum's.

JAMIE: Who's this the road sweeper?

TONY: Shut up. Thing is mate we're expecting someone. A guest. You must have past them if you come up Essex Road?

NAT: I came round the back.

TONY: Yeah, of course.

Enter CAROL – stage right.

JAMIE: It's the road sweeper!

TONY: I told you! It's Bill's dad.

CAROL: Oh hello. They've gone.

TONY: I've said that.

CAROL: We're busy!

NAT: Billy's phoned and –

CAROL: You order the food?

JAMIE: You told me to answer the door didn't you!

TONY: Look mate we ain't got time for this right now.

CAROL: We've got a guest, for dinner.

NAT: It won't take long.

CAROL: Are you fucking dense or what?

Offstage – the door bell rings.

JAMIE: Shall I get it?

CAROL: Hold up. Tone?

TONY: Come and play the concerned dad tomorrow alright?

NAT: Not really.

The door bell rings – again.

CAROL: We can't leave him out there all night. Jamie get the door.

JAMIE exits – stage right.

TONY: What about him?

CAROL: He can go out the back way.

TONY: Come on you, lively.

NAT: Don't be touching me.

Enter EMMA, BILLY and JAMIE.

CAROL: Thought you were going – never mind. Get rid of him will you?

EMMA: What do you want?

NAT: So many things.

JAMIE: He's mad!

CAROL: I thought you were taking him to his Nan's anyway?

EMMA: We couldn't get a cab.

TONY: Round here at this time of night?

EMMA: I've only got seven pounds in cash and –

JAMIE: Oh no, she ain't got enough for a cab!

BILLY: In cash! We didn't know if Nan'd be at home or at the club.

NAT: I can run you up after this. If you want.

CAROL: It's only Bill, Emma's staying here.

NAT: Fine. How are you Billy?

BILLY: I'm fine. I saw the van.

CAROL: He'll be here in a minute.

TONY: You got to go mate.

CAROL: Can't you see we're busy?

JAMIE: So go on, fuck off. What you think I'm joking?

NAT: Think you'd better be.

CAROL: Tone.

TONY: I could make a call and you'd wish you'd have gone son.

CAROL: We know who you owe money.

NAT: Personally? I didn't think so.

CAROL: He knows people don't worry about that.

NAT: I paid them.

TONY: Not what I heard.

NAT: No, it wouldn't be.

TONY: Anyway with them it's not the money it's the principle.

NAT: Actually with them, it's the other way around.

JAMIE: They'll blow your fucking brains out.

NAT: That'll be messy.

CAROL: Tone, we've only just had the carpets done.

TONY: I'll get them to wait outside for you.

NAT: Then you'd have to talk to me anyway.

TONY: Yeah 'cos you're hanging around once I've picked up that phone.

NAT: Yep.

TONY: You what?

NAT: Try me.

JAMIE: I'll try you. I'll call Chilli. He knows them! They'll rip you open like a bag of crisps. You mug.

TONY: Not in this house they won't. Got it?

CAROL: We've got to get rid of him?

NAT: If it's Brownie points you're after, ring them when I'm leaving.

TONY: Brownie – I'm not like that! I'm not am I Carol. People round here treat them like they're The Sopranos but I don't. We're not like that, we don't even mention them.

BILLY: Yes you do. Often.

TONY: Not compared to the rest of them round here – honestly! Look, can't this wait? We're expecting someone important.

NAT: Oh yeah, of course you are.

EMMA: What have you been saying Billy?

BILLY: Nothing.

JAMIE: Shit! I'll see you later.

TONY: Oi, Jamie mate. Who the fuck's Chinney?

JAMIE: Chilli! They like him.

CAROL: Jesus Christ.

TONY: Be careful son.

JAMIE: I don't knock about with him.

TONY: You'd fucking better not be. I'm telling you.

JAMIE: What am I supposed to do, blank him?

TONY: You do what I do, keep them sweet – from a distance.

JAMIE: Yeah alright.

TONY: What's that supposed to mean?

JAMIE: You loved it when one of them was going to buy that house across the street. You thought you were going to get in with them.

TONY: What are you mad. That's the last thing I want to do!

JAMIE: Whatever. I'm bouncing.

TONY: You're what? Rartie bumper clart mon!

CAROL: Tone?

TONY: That's not racist! Anyway you, What's wrong with your one-tens?

JAMIE: Don't go with me Evisu's, party's more Grungy anyway.

TONY: Didn't say that in the shop! You'll have all this Emma – honestly. Got your phone? Said goodbye to mummy?

JAMIE: See you later mum.

Exit JAMIE – stage right.

TONY: Home by one okay?

The front door slams – off.

CAROL: I'll phone him later make sure he's alright.

TONY: See, got all different mates and that. Tonight's are more middle classy, what he meant by grungy one-tens are trainers cost that much, what they call them.

NAT: You retain stuff like that?

EMMA: Where's, Paul?

TONY: You know what the traffic's like round here Fridays.

CAROL: He ain't going to show.

TONY: He just called you silly cow.

CAROL: You want to have a bet? I'll give you a pound to a penny.

TONY: Pound to a, I'll call him!… It's switched off.

CAROL: I knew he was going to do this.

TONY: Do what? He might have got the wrong street or something.

CAROL: Fucking knew it.

EMMA: Might have been nice if you'd have mentioned it to me.

CAROL: I didn't – know, know.

TONY: What? What's going on here?

NAT: Go and wait upstairs Billy. Please.

Exit BILLY – stage right.

TONY: Well?

CAROL: Asked me out once. Before I was seeing you, I stood him up.

TONY: Oh yeah, whole world revolves around you Carol. Can you believe this? He's probably had a million birds since then. He's an award winning advert director, sure to be harbouring a grudge against you for a quarter of a century! He probably didn't turn up his'self?

CAROL: He did, my mate saw him standing outside the pictures. He'd phoned the night before you know, to confirm it. It was my sister –

TONY: Odd on she'd have something to do with it.

CAROL: She kept saying he was alright. But you know, she played table tennis.

TONY: Why didn't you – Emma's shelled out for a new dress! We've done a hundred quid –

CAROL: It's not a hundred! We can eat it in the week Tone.

TONY: What about that Thai, what's that going to come to?

EMMA: Have we actually ordered that?

CAROL: No.

TONY: You couldn't even get that together?

CAROL: Oh fuck off.

EMMA: You could have forewarned me Carol?

CAROL: Wasn't sure if he'd remember and it was a good part. For Jamie. It was going to be like the Oxo family.

EMMA: It was an advert?

TONY: We know people who've bought houses off of adverts don't worry about that! Only an advert. See, honestly.

CAROL: Civilians.

NAT: Excuse me?

TONY: Nothing.

CAROL: Fancy another one Emma? Nat, drink?

NAT: Cup of tea'd be nice.

CAROL: Tea? Don't you want a beer or something?

EMMA: Carol?

CAROL: Oh sorry! Tone?

TONY: You can't drink either? Knew you were a junkie but. Well I suppose if you can't handle it. I'll have a lager please.

Exit CAROL – stage left.

EMMA: I don't remember you having a drink problem?

TONY: Ain't going to make it up to impress people is he! Not even a puff of a joint?

NAT: Nope.

TONY: This all part of your what's it, cult?

NAT: Cult? It's the Twelve Step Programme. It works.

EMMA: All that praying seems cultish to me.

TONY: Didn't you say he had to live in a special place and that?

NAT: Bournemouth?

TONY: The thingy where you weren't allowed to speak to anyone outside?

NAT: They didn't say I wasn't allowed to speak to anyone.

EMMA: That's where Nat met God – in treatment.

TONY: What was he in for?

EMMA: Control issues.

Enter CAROL with drinks.

TONY: You knocking on people's doors now banging on about Jesus?

CAROL: Jesus – I thought you were Jewish?

Police sirens are heard off.

TONY: Sounds a bit close?

CAROL: (*At window.*) Something's gone off across the street.

EMMA: It's hard to imagine anything ever happening in there.

CAROL: It's an Irish pub Emma. Be Paddies fighting I suppose.

TONY: Get away from the window, look like a fish wife. Here are, sip of beer him, falls apart.

CAROL: Sad ain't it. Oh I forgot your tea! I'll do it in a minute.

NAT: Shall we get this sorted out?

EMMA: I need a holiday. We both do.

NAT: He comes down to Bourn–

EMMA: Abroad. Just because you're stuck down there doesn't mean he has to be.

NAT: I'm not stuck. I'll leave when I'm ready.

EMMA: When are they going to tell you that? It's been two years.

NAT: I don't need permission. If you want a foreign holiday, save up like everyone else.

TONY: Fuck me – she's on the social mate! What? You just gave her a look?

NAT: I did didn't I.

CAROL: Been right looking forward to this holiday Emma has.

TONY: Bill might have his doubts but once he gets there he's going to love it. I know he's not trendy but you know, nice to tell his mates he's been to Ibiza. Honestly.

NAT: Ibiza?

TONY: Not San Antonio.

CAROL: That's the muggy part.

TONY: Ibiza Town. The ream – good part.

NAT: I don't need any Balearic geography lessons from you.

EMMA: We met in Pasha. It's a club.

TONY: I know what it is. We, we went there – honestly. Didn't we!

CAROL: Few years ago.

NAT: Oh they doing coach trips now?

CAROL: What's so funny Emma?

TONY: I was going to flash clubs while you were still at school.

NAT: So was I.

TONY: He'd better be back by one Carol – honestly.

NAT: I'm not having this. Billy taking the blame. It's insane.

TONY: You don't want him to do it. Don't bother us – seriously.

CAROL: Awkward getting someone else sorted by Monday Tone?

TONY: Yeah that's all it'll be, awkward. I don't know what you're making such a fuss about Nat. It's a slap on the wrist.

NAT: I suspect misogyny's treated more seriously than that.

CAROL: Misogyny?

NAT: What would you call breaking into the girls changing rooms and scattering their underwear all over the playground?

CAROL: A laugh.

TONY: Resent them having a holiday, that's the price they'll pay.

EMMA: I've got enough money to live alright but not for things like holidays Nat.

NAT: No one does, that's why they save. I could cover a fortnight in Ibiza anyway.

TONY: Some crappy one yeah. This gaff's a bit exclusive.

NAT: They let you in.

TONY: Only, only 'cos my pal's got an apartment.

CAROL: You might end up in San Antonio Emma, surrounded by fat blokes in Leeds football shirts.

NAT: Or you can be surrounded by cabbies pretending to be gangsters.

TONY: No, no! My pal's brother was in Spandel Ballet!

NAT: I think I'd prefer the Leeds shirts.

EMMA: I wouldn't.

TONY: Make your mind up Emma. Jamie'd take the blame himself but he's been in a spot of trouble before. Only kids stuff but –

CAROL: He's on a warning.

NAT: He'll be expelled?

CAROL: Excluded they call it now.

TONY: I don't know if they'd go that far. Be good for Bill, socially, word gets around he's helped Jamie out.

CAROL: He's one of the chaps see – Jamie.

NAT: Letting his parents get involved? He wouldn't have been one of the chaps at my school.

CAROL: Oh yeah and where did you go?

NAT: Holloway.

TONY: Misogynistic Jamie? World's gone mad. It was a prank.

CAROL: Did a lot worse in my day. I tell you what, you should hear some of the filth that comes out of their mouths, then you wouldn't think they were so bleeding innocent!

NAT: Are you saying Jamie knew these girls, that it was premeditated?

CAROL: No! Girls these days, they're different. I get on the bus when they're going to school, I hear them.

TONY: And don't start on about the Paki, if she was so religious, what was she doing swimming in the first place?

NAT: Why don't you blame the school for having a pool?

CAROL: What?

NAT: How the fuck did you get mixed up with these?

TONY: These? These! Rich coming from a junkie.

CAROL: We've been helping her out.

NAT: Pimping her out.

TONY: Pimp – she's gagging for it. Don't deny it, said didn't she!

EMMA: Who's denying anything?

TONY: No wonder the kid's weird.

NAT: Easy now.

TONY: Don't get out of your pram sunshine 'cos I'm half warming to the thought of –

Enter BILLY stage right. He holds the Playstation box.

BILLY: I don't want this Tony. You should get your money back.

TONY: It's up to you Bill?

EMMA: It was a kind gesture Tony.

NAT: It might have been if it were something he actually wanted.

BILLY: What time are we going? I'm hungry.

CAROL: I'll make you something. Fancy a mini pork pie? Hold on.

Exit CAROL – stage left.

BILLY: Did you sort, sort things out with Georgie?

NAT: Yeah. I've got a couple of things to tie up down there before I can move but it won't take long.

EMMA: Georgie?

NAT: We're going to work together.

EMMA: But you, you can't fight Nat? Not now.

TONY: Fight?

Enter CAROL – stage left.

CAROL: I put some crisps round. Makes it nice.

BILLY: Thank you. So it's definite, you're coming back?

NAT: Definite. Within the month. Go up Billy, we'll call you.

Exit BILLY – stage right.

Personal Training. I've done a few courses and you know, I'm training all the time anyway.

TONY: Did a bit of boxing did you?

NAT: Kickboxing. I did Tai Kwon Do for years so…

TONY: Kick boxer, what professional?

NAT: Of sorts.

EMMA: Could have been the champion.

NAT: I could have been a contender… It was you Charlie, that night at the garden, you said, this ain't your night kid. Not my night?

CAROL: What's he on about, who's Charlie?

TONY: It's De Niro at the end of Raging Bull.

CAROL: Why weren't you then? Anyone can say they could have been this or that can't they.

EMMA: Our lifestyle didn't help much.

NAT: Or the money.

TONY: Being skint's supposed to spur fighters on ain't it?

EMMA: Who said anything about being skint?

NAT: No I did alright out of the old Acid House.

TONY: Anyone can get a few quid drug dealing.

EMMA: He wasn't a dealer.

NAT: I promoted raves. Had a radio station at one point.

TONY: Pirate!

EMMA: And a record label.

NAT: Long gone.

TONY: While you were fucking about we were investing in Canonbury. Forty-five grand we give for that.

NAT: Maybe we should have invested more?

EMMA: And miss all that spending?

NAT: That odyssey of grandiosity. I'll never know how far I could have got with the fighting. That's a regret.

TONY: All got regrets, all could have been something.

NAT: Oh yeah – what could you have been?

CAROL: I could have been an actress.

TONY: That'll be fifty-five pence please. Four years at Anna's for that?

CAROL: At the end I was getting auditions, you didn't like it.

TONY: Only, only because of your tits! I need that – see your Carol on Benny Hill the other night Tone.

CAROL: Yeah you don't mind with Alice though do you!

EMMA: (*Indicating portrait.*) Their daughter.

NAT: What is she a Page Three or something?

CAROL: Fucking cheek – she's a presenter! Britain's favourite morning pop host.

TONY: That's a fact. Won the Telly Quick Award for it.

NAT: Oh yeah – The Pop Files!

CAROL: That's it.

EMMA: You watch breakfast TV?

NAT: In the cafe. Before work.

EMMA: I never imagined you working. Just sitting in meeting's talking about, your issues.

TONY: We've got a cafe! Nice one though. Phone rings, fellow behind the ramp calls out a hotel, up gets a cabbie – walks out. People like you'd sit there wondering what's going on. Airport jobs, know what I mean? Good ain't it, sit there chatting, or reading a book – drive round to a hotel, up the airport, fare back in… Couple of those a day and you've got your two hundred quid. Gets a grand a week. Enough though ain't it.

NAT: Apparently not.

TONY: Alright, alright – how much were you getting doing those raves?

EMMA: Considerably more than that.

TONY: I've got a two bed in Canonbury as well as this you know?

CAROL: Our tenants are barristers.

TONY: Can't work it out – paying rent to a cabbie – honestly. We went to a couple of those raves.

CAROL: No we didn't.

TONY: With Kenny that time, at the Scarla.

CAROL: That was a warehouse party. We never went to any of those Acid dos. Alice was a toddler when that came out Tone.

EMMA: It was an amazing thing. You would have loved it Carol.

TONY: No she wouldn't, she's not a freak.

EMMA: No?

TONY: She's normal, we're normal. Normal London people! I'm a bit shrewd and that, she's not. We balance out – normal. See you, you thought you were clever and ended up sticking fucking needles in your arm, that's how clever you were. You've probably got fucking Aids!

NAT: That's right HIV. Happy Pappy?

CAROL: Jesus Tony. I'll get your tea, it's already boiled so...

TONY: I didn't know did I!

CAROL: Didn't you? You're the fucking shrewd nut!

CAROL hits TONY on her way out.

Exit CAROL – stage left.

TONY: I swear I didn't, don't look like you've got it. Mind you nor does Mark Fowler.

NAT: The footballer?

TONY: No. Off EastEnders. Know he ain't really got it but they use make up. Do the eyes all dark and, I tell you what –

EMMA: For God's sake man – shut up.

TONY: What about you, you know?

NAT: No she hasn't.

TONY: Bill?

EMMA: No!

TONY: That's alright.

NAT: Worried about your toilet seat?

Enter CAROL – stage left.

CAROL: Here are love.

She hands NAT tea and biscuits.

NAT: Cheers.

Silence.

TONY: No wonder he's all deep. I'd be like that living with a death sentence over me.

CAROL: Would you?

TONY: Course. Emma and Bill are alright.

CAROL: Yeah I heard.

TONY: How long you got then?

EMMA: Is this a nervous thing?

NAT: Got a while. God willing.

TONY: Can do all the make up and but he was still fat. Mark Fowler.

CAROL: Not going to lose weight for the part, it's a soap!

EMMA: I think Nat's right, about Billy.

TONY: Fine.

CAROL: What about Jamie?

TONY: We'll sort something out.

CAROL: We'd better. By the way Nat, I think you're right brave.

TONY: He ain't a fireman! Not being funny but you know, reap what you sow don't you.

NAT: Yep.

TONY searches his address book.

TONY: Can I speak to Donovan please? – Oh it's you. You're voice's got deeper. It's Jamie's dad – hold up! Fancy earning yourself a hundred, no two hundred quid Monday morning? – All you got to do is go up the school – He's got an Exclusion Order from the school.

CAROL: Offer that Playstation and all.

TONY: Listen, listen, we'll throw in a PS2, all the top games, been chipped so – Right, you just go to the Headmaster's office and say it was you that flung some girls' underwear around the playground. – I swear that's it. – Definitely? – Get round here tomorrow I'll give you the details… Didn't even say goodbye. So ignorant ain't they? What we should have done in the first place this.

CAROL: I said that!

TONY: Yeah alright. What?

NAT: How's Jamie going to learn to take responsibility for his actions while you keep pulling stunts like this?

TONY: Food chain! Food chain! That's all he's got to understand!

NAT: You're a sick man you know that? Plus you're a fucking moron.

TONY: Moron! Moron? I'm not the one –

CAROL: Tony! Please. I've had enough arguing for one night.

The phone rings.

TONY: That's Paul let me speak to him.

CAROL: Alright Teen. He didn't turn up. Having a hen night Nat.

TONY: Married an' all half of them – honestly.

CAROL: Emma they've booked a stripper – No! He's called Oscar 'cause he's a foot long! – Hang on. She wants to know if you're going to meet up with them Em?

EMMA: No. Not tonight.

CAROL: She says not tonight. – Me? Don't be daft! See you later.

TONY: She ask you to go? Liberty.

EMMA: I'll get Billy.

CAROL: Time Emma. Why don't we make a night of it anyway? Be here in twenty minutes.

TONY: What are you – mad?

CAROL: Why not? Don't you fancy a bit of Thai Nat? Emma?

EMMA: I am hungry.

NAT: I don't know Carol. Shouldn't we be getting Billy around to my mum's?

EMMA: He stays up late on Karaoke nights. I'll get him.

Exit EMMA – stage right.

CAROL: Maybe you could drop him off and come back Nat. No offence but I'd like to have a night without any kids wrapped around me. Come on be nice, a little Dinner Party.

TONY: Carol, they don't even like us.

CAROL: They don't mind me! Nat?

NAT: Sorry Carol.

TONY: Siddy Smith went Holloway didn't he?

NAT: Same year.

Enter EMMA – stage right.

EMMA: He's fast asleep. I tried to wake him but…

CAROL: If he's dead to the world?

NAT: What's it like? Bad Thai's horrendous. Sorry?

TONY: Bit of a connoisseur then?

NAT: I wouldn't go that far.

TONY: Sounds like it. Been Soho Thai have you?

NAT: Did we?

EMMA: No.

TONY: Don't know what you're talking about then. Best gaff in London. Dropping punters at top restaurants all day long.

CAROL: He is.

TONY: Name your best Thai, come on.

NAT: This is ridiculous.

TONY: See – he don't even know any! Hate bad Thai.

NAT: What do you think, Kim's? Kim's Noodle House.

TONY: Never heard of it. Where's that – Ruislip?

NAT: Bangkok.

TONY: Jamie better be back by one Carol – honestly.

CAROL: You'd better pick him up then. When did you find out Nat, you know?

NAT: In treatment.

CAROL: Must have been a bit rough?

NAT: A touch yeah.

TONY: How come you ain't got it then?

NAT: We'd stopped playing happy families by that time.

CAROL: Well you're alright now?

TONY: Could make a night of it, why not?

CAROL: Oh Tone! You order while I get changed then.

Exit CAROL – stage right.

EMMA: Where's that menu? Let me see what they've got.

EMMA sits on the sofa and studies the menu.

TONY: Follow the football?

NAT: Not really. Chelsea sort of.

TONY: West Ham. Season ticket.

EMMA: This looks really good.

NAT: I'd have thought you'd have been Arsenal around here?

TONY: The old man was West Ham. Proper London club.

NAT: Losers? Talking of dad's, mine gave me that bike.

TONY: What bike?

NAT: Billy's bike.

TONY: Whoa! Billy did alright out of that. One we give him's different class to the one that broke.

NAT: Broke? It was feeling a bit tired in the shed there, and broke?

TONY: Alright Jamie was messing about but –

NAT: Messing about – he smashed it with a hammer!

TONY: They, they shouldn't have the bike shed next to the Metalwork room! I bet that's not the first time something like that's happened – honestly.

NAT: It's almost entrapment really.

EMMA: How did you get our address?

TONY: Carol knows someone in the office. At the school. Fuck me you can't blame us for going round there, they were talking about getting the police involved!

NAT: And romance blossomed.

TONY: That Headmaster's got a lot to answer for. You can't have kid's arrested for stuff like that, this is Islington. Might have got all trendy that school but there's plenty of working class kids there, and they, they get resentful. Even you must understand that?

NAT: But it's not as if Jamie's from an economically or socially deprived back –

TONY: Oh and that'd make it alright would it? Typical that is!

NAT: But… He's schizophrenic.

EMMA: I know.

TONY: He's not. I'm not – honestly. I'll be back in a minute.

Exit TONY – stage right.

NAT: He's sort of remarkable in a way. You know Emma, if you'd wanted to see me all you had to do was say.

EMMA: I tried once, I was told you were too vulnerable to come to the phone…when they came around about the bike.

NAT: I'd just been diagnosed.

EMMA: How was I supposed to know?

NAT: I wrote and told you.

EMMA: Three months later. Which, by the way, was a nice letter to receive after over a year of waiting.

NAT: I was advised against getting in touch with you for the first twelve months.

EMMA: No one's allowed to speak to their partners for a year?

NAT: Some are but I was advised against it in your case.

EMMA: You were no stroll in the park yourself Nat.

NAT: I know but I've been trying to turn it around.

EMMA: So am I, I'm hardly close to the edge here.

NAT: I'm not so sure. What's this all about anyway?

EMMA: They adopted me. No one else has taken too much interest. Nobody manageable anyway.

Enter TONY – stage right.

TONY: Won't be a minute.

Exit TONY – stage left.

Enter TONY – stage left carrying a large torch.

Exit TONY – stage right.

NAT: You told them you didn't have any money?

EMMA: No they made that presumption. They make lots of them.

NAT: I was hoping we might have gone out for a meal tonight.

EMMA: With Billy?

NAT: No.

EMMA: Oh, right.

NAT: How would you have been with that?

EMMA: Fine. Glad.

NAT: Really? Oh, right.

Enter CAROL – stage right all dolled up.

CAROL: What do you reckon? Where's he?

NAT: He came in a second ago, for a torch.

CAROL: He's in the cab… oh I know. He order?

EMMA: I don't know. You look amazing Carol.

CAROL: No need to sound so surprised. Bit of a squeeze.

EMMA: I don't think he has ordered.

NAT: Not to my knowledge.

Enter TONY – stage right.

TONY: On its way is it?

CAROL: You were supposed to order it!

TONY: Alright, alright. Who wants another drink?

CAROL: Me and Emma are on vodka and orange.

TONY: Nat, orange juice, Diet Coke?

NAT: Yeah cheers, Diet please.

Exit TONY – stage left.

CAROL studies the menu.

CAROL: Got a thing, a set meal here. Get that for four eh?

NAT: I'm not sure we're staying.

CAROL: But – Emma?

EMMA: Perhaps we could eat here and you go back
  tomorrow?

CAROL: Make your mind up Nat, I want to ring them.

NAT: I could go back tomorrow.

CAROL: Good. Tone I'm getting the set meal!

NAT: Wow.

CAROL: You hear me?

TONY: (*Off.*) How do you get this ice out? Carol!

CAROL: He's useless I swear. Hold up! Oh hello, I'd like to
  order the set meal for four. – Cash. 44 Lambert Street,
  it's off – Do you? – 7607 1989. – Cheers. He knew the
  street.

Exit CAROL stage left.

EMMA: Are you okay?

NAT: No yeah, I'm…it's what I'd hoped for.

*EMMA reaches out and touches NAT but withdraws her
hand as enter TONY – stage left carrying a tray of drinks.*

TONY: She's bringing the ice. Here are Nat.

NAT: Cheers.

TONY: Emma.

EMMA: Thank you.

TONY: Come on Carol!

CAROL: (*Off.*) I'm coming!

Enter CAROL – stage left carrying a jug of ice.

TONY: The ice maker's broken. On the fridge.

CAROL: That was Jamie messing about with it. Let's have a toast – the future!

TONY: Bit insensitive ain't it?

CAROL: What?

TONY: Him!

NAT: Me? I'm fine with the future Tony.

TONY: Right, the future.

ALL: The future!

CAROL: Nice ain't it. Being nice.

TONY: You ordered that scran?

CAROL: Yes!

TONY: Good.

EMMA: Tony! What are you doing?

TONY: Chopping out lines cocaine.

EMMA: And you're accusing Carol of insensitivity?

TONY: Not with you?

EMMA: Is that not a little unthinking?

NAT: I'd imagine Tony's given it plenty of thought.

TONY: Slow down – what's that meant to mean? Here are, Carol?

CAROL: We got it for tonight. With Paul and that.

TONY: And Emma, fancy a line don't you. Just 'cos he can't, don't mean the rest of us have to suffer does it.

EMMA: I'd hardly call it suffering. I've gone without for two years and haven't missed it. Impressed?

NAT: I think your pathology'd find addiction a trifle mundane.

CAROL: I'm not missing out.

TONY: Two?

CAROL: Well she's not having any is she. Mental buzz ain't it.

TONY: I'm having a little one, make it last. Cor that hits the spot.

NAT: You should trying mixing it up with a bit of smack and injecting it.

TONY: Did you a lot of good.

CAROL: Yeah when I phoned they knew the street and everything. Getting double trendy round here now ain't it.

TONY: Still bomb-damaged from the Blitz when I was a kid this street – honestly.

CAROL: Decimated Hoxton that. Where me mum's from.

NAT: So you've both lived around here all your lives?

CAROL: Around here? He was born in here. Not this room – obviously. He had three bedrooms growing up, used to alternate them didn't you.

NAT: Really?

TONY: What's wrong with that? They bought in the sixties. The old man was a florist – proper one though, had to know what you were doing back then. No refrigerated lorries and all that. He's gone to me – be all yours one day this. I thought yeah cheers. It was all dark and damp. All me mates had cozy little council flats with central heating and white walls. I was right envious, I was honestly! Mad ain't it.

CAROL: Used to tell people he was from the Packington.

TONY: Yeah that was just, I aligned myself with them, had to be in firm growing up around here. You don't want any?

EMMA: No thank you.

CAROL: Oh it's mental gear. Put the telly on, have some music.

NAT: The telly.

CAROL: Yeah we got MTV and that. He don't really like music.

TONY: Yes I do!

CAROL: Wouldn't buy a stereo.

TONY: Kids have got one each. Don't need three do we!

CAROL: Got five tellys. You got a stereo Emma? See even she's got one!

NAT: Even?

CAROL: Yeah. I mean she's skint but she's still got a stereo.

NAT: She's not.

CAROL: What? Why she say she has then?

NAT: She's not skint.

TONY: Not now, got her that job down the bakery.

NAT: Emma doesn't need to work down the bakery.

TONY: No she does it for amusement!

CAROL: We've been helping her – he's even got Bill a computer thing.

NAT: I suspect that had little to do with helping Billy.

TONY: I suppose you've got a darker, twisted version have you?

NAT: I suspect you're threatened by Billy's contentment with his antiquated console, his daring to be different.

CAROL: Fucking hell!

TONY: He is mad?

EMMA: I don't know Tony, is he?

CAROL: You, you go along with it then Em?

EMMA: He was threatened by my shoes earlier.

TONY: No, no – isn't Johnny Moke better than L K Bennett?

NAT: Are these more soap characters?

TONY: They're shoes for fucksake!

EMMA: Ladies' shoes.

TONY: Getting to see the other side of you now. After all we've done an' all.

EMMA: You haven't done that much.

TONY: See, some people it's never enough. I've helped you right out.

EMMA: Carol got me the job.

The door bell rings.

TONY: Who is it – Paul Thornton?

CAROL: No. It's some black geezer. What's he want?

TONY: I don't know do I! Go and find out.

CAROL: Me – he might be a lunatic or something.

The door bell rings again.

TONY: Answer the door will you!

CAROL: Alright!

Exit CAROL – stage right.

TONY: I told her to get you that job as it happens.

EMMA: Thanks.

TONY: Don't know why I bothered now.

EMMA: You didn't enjoy being my knight in shinning armour?

TONY: Fuck me it was only part time.

Enter CAROL – stage right.

CAROL: He's a traffic warden. Where's my purse, give me forty quid will you? Now!

TONY: Slow down.

CAROL: Slow down? Jamie's told him he'll get forty quid for delivering a message.

TONY: I'm not having this.

Exit TONY and CAROL – stage right.

EMMA: What do you think?

NAT: Traffic Wardens work out of police stations.

EMMA: He's been arrested? This is great! I wonder what for?

NAT: I don't know Emma. I don't know if it's great either.

EMMA: No you don't.

Offstage the front door slams.

TONY: (*Off.*) Because he's a fucking idiot Carol!

CAROL: (*Off.*) Tone.

Enter CAROL & TONY – stage right.

EMMA: What's wrong?

TONY: He's only gone and got himself nicked! That's it Carol, I'm finished with him – honestly.

CAROL: We don't know if he did it yet.

EMMA: Did what?

CAROL: Nothing.

NAT: What's he been accused of?

CAROL: We don't know yet.

TONY: Yes we do, drug dealing. He's been nicked for drug dealing!

CAROL: He could lose the series.

NAT: He could lose his liberty. Drug dealing.

CAROL: He's only sixteen!

NAT: Might give him the old Short Sharp Shock. Three months of marching – at the double.

TONY: Do him good the spoilt bastard.

CAROL: I can see him buying drugs.

TONY: That's illegal Carol.

CAROL: Yeah but there's a big difference between buying them and selling them ain't there Nat.

TONY: He's a prick. Always has been.

EMMA: Rather harsh Tony?

TONY: Been the same since Nursery – he's the one who gets caught. You know how many times I've been nicked? Never. I've got a bit of guile though.

CAROL: This is about Jamie not you! That Traffic Warden reckoned the Old Bill expected to be charging the other fellow?

TONY: Yeah, yeah. Who's he with then?

CAROL: Stevie – played Trigger's brother in Fools and Horses.

TONY: Different class Fools and Horses. Bit old to be knocking about with Jamie him?

CAROL: You know what it is, he's been done for drugs before and –

TONY: Jamie's helping him out!

CAROL: You know what he's like for his mates and that.

TONY: It's right. He's as soft as shit – honestly.

CAROL: Fuck this. I'm going up there, make sure he's not being bullied into it. 'Cos that's a fucking liberty.

TONY: What's the point, he's nicked. What?

NAT: I don't think they can charge him without an adult present.

CAROL: But the Traffic –

TONY: He knows more than some fucking Traffic Warden! Right – you get up there I'll phone Kenny. There's some brief that they use – supposed to be shit hot. Solomon I think it is. What you doing?

CAROL: Having a line. Need a bit of a boost. I'll see you in a minute.

TONY: You've done half of it!

CAROL: Should have got more then shouldn't you!

TONY: You'll create a good impression!

EMMA: You've got coke all around your nose.

CAROL: Better? I'll see you later.

Exit CAROL – stage right.

TONY: Kenny give me a ring soon as, bit agg this end mate. He must have copped for a bird or something.

Enter BILLY – stage right.

EMMA: Hello sleepy head. Do you want to go and see Nana at the club?

BILLY: Sleepy head? She might be wondering where I am.

NAT: Come on then. Got all your stuff?

TONY: Not going yet are you – what about the Thai?

EMMA: Haven't you got more pressing matters Tony?

TONY: What about me? Can't you wait until she gets back?

NAT: We don't know how long she's going to be Tony.

TONY: Police station's only up the road there?

NAT: That's not really the point.

BILLY: What's going on?

TONY: Nothing.

NAT: Jamie's been arrested.

BILLY: What for?

TONY: Nothing.

BILLY: Has he put a cap in someone?

TONY: What – hold up – he's grinning!

EMMA: Drug dealing.

TONY: Oi! It's not fucking funny!

NAT: Billy? Can you show some discretion?

BILLY: I'm sorry but, I'm sorry.

TONY: Perhaps you'd better go.

EMMA: I've left some stuff upstairs. Christ Tony you can't be surprised, Jamie's not very nice. To Billy anyway.

TONY: Lets him play on his games and that doesn't he.

EMMA: Only because he had to.

BILLY: I did 'Tie a Yellow Ribbon' last week. Karaoke.

EMMA: Okay. I'll get my stuff.

Exit EMMA – stage right.

TONY: Think he's dealing drugs Bill?

BILLY: I don't know. I think he would have boasted about it.

TONY: See what Kenny's got to say – phone's off. Don't stop rumping his fares. Only young and all some of them. You know, twenties and that. I think he's lonely really. Here Nat, reckon if the Cozzers fancy this other geezer, they'll let me have a word with Jame, talk some sense into him?

NAT: Maybe.

TONY: Don't sound too convinced?

NAT: Is this other bloke well known or something, as an actor?

TONY: No. They were in a Government Health Warning together.

BILLY: Who was he?

TONY: The teacher.

BILLY: He was good.

TONY: Yeah don't get much work. He's far from well known.

NAT: Then why would Jamie help him out?

BILLY: He wouldn't.

TONY: He might. He's, he a nice kid really. Deep down.

Enter EMMA – stage right.

EMMA: Okay, that's it.

TONY: You, you going?

NAT: It's a police station Tony, she could be hours.

TONY: Couldn't you wait five minutes. We've got loads of food?

NAT: We'll give it a few minutes.

BILLY: Dad?

EMMA: Are you hungry?

BILLY: Are there any more of those mini pork pies?

TONY: Yeah help yourself.

EMMA: I'll make some tea.

Exit EMMA – stage left.

TONY: None for me Emma! Bill you know you said about him boasting about it – if he was at it –

BILLY: He probably would.

TONY: I make you right. There's something wrong here 'cos he wouldn't take the nick for someone like Trigger's brother either.

NAT: Hadn't you better get a solicitor on board?

TONY: Do you know any? This what's it, Solomon I think it is, he's the one. Kenny'd know. Oh Jamie you fucking idiot. You can have a go on the X-Box if you want Bill.

BILLY: Oh right.

NAT: Stay here. Your mum's making you some tea.

EMMA: (*Off.*) We're going to have trouble getting a table anywhere if we leave it too late.

NAT: We'll be fine.

BILLY: You're going out, what about me?

NAT: You're staying at Nan's.

TONY: Out on a date? Well she's all dressed up for it.

NAT: Lucky me eh Tony?

TONY: Are you? I don't know.

EMMA: (*Off.*) Billy if you want any biscuits you'd better come and choose.

BILLY: Coming.

Exit BILLY – stage left.

TONY: Untold Personal Trainers about these days though ain't there. Hard supporting a family?

NAT: We'll survive.

TONY: Want to do a bit more than that though don't you. Anyway, you won't, not for long. Don't you want to leave him something Bill?

NAT: He'll get the flat and –

TONY: You can't say – council might move him out. Say it's under occupied?

93

NAT: It's got nothing to do with the council. We bought off them about fifteen years ago.

Enter EMMA and BILLY – stage left.

EMMA: I presume you haven't started taking sugar?

NAT: No.

TONY: You didn't tell me you owned that flat?

EMMA: You didn't ask. Biscuit?

TONY: Social been paying your mortgage? Fucking joke that is.

EMMA: There's no mortgage. We bought it outright. Cash.

TONY: You what?

BILLY: Yes!

NAT: Rave promotions was pretty cash based.

TONY: How much you give for it then?

NAT: Not much. I got a fair old discount, I'd been there a few years.

TONY: I – got any more little surprises for me?

BILLY: My grandfather's rich.

TONY: Oh rich is he? Who's this your old man?

NAT: My dad's dead.

TONY: So's, so's mine!

NAT: Emma's stepfather.

EMMA: He's well off, he's not wealthy.

BILLY: He was in The Sunday Times Rich List!

TONY: Straight?

EMMA: Barely. I think he was ninety-sixth.

TONY: Yeah still more than just well off. I'm well – you could have said?

EMMA: Why? They get on my nerves.

NAT: Not enough to turn down your fifteen grand a year allowance.

EMMA: I'm not stupid. Anyway since they paid for your treatment and set up Billy's Trust Fund –

TONY: Trust Fund! Fucking Trust Fund! Are you sure?

EMMA: Aren't your properties a Trust Fund of sorts Tony?

TONY: You've been, been taking the piss out of us you.

EMMA: I think any piss-taking's been a two way street. Don't you?

TONY: We've been helping you out.

EMMA: I thought you rather enjoyed having me around?

TONY: Been company for Carol I suppose.

EMMA: You suppose right.

TONY: Yeah, what's that meant to mean?

EMMA: Mean? Nothing. Why what do you think it meant?

TONY: You're not like what's it are you – aristocracy?

EMMA: No!

TONY: Thank fuck for that.

NAT: You don't go for them?

TONY: It's not that… I just would have felt even more of a mug. What is he, in the City?

EMMA: He's a long way from the City. Billy?

BILLY: I'm just an ordinary Scouser made good.

TONY: Scouser! A rich Scouser? There's no such thing!

EMMA: You'd like him, he's a bit of a wide boy.

BILLY: He's not, he's a property developer!

TONY: Fuck off – you can buy a street up there for a fiver!
No you can, it was in the paper – honestly!

BILLY: The Sun?

TONY: Leave it out. It was in one of them. Fucking Trust
Funds and rich Scousers? They're all skint everyone
knows that.

NAT: Ged Duffy seems to be doing alright.

TONY: What you doing in the bakery if you've got money?

EMMA: I get an allowance, it's hardly – having money.

NAT: Billy'll be okay though. He paid for me treatment.

TONY: Billy?

NAT: Ged. Not cheap.

EMMA: I still think that was to split us up.

TONY: Where's she? What was all that bollocks about
earlier with the Playstation. Can't someone just do
something kind?

NAT: I doubt if you can.

TONY: I drive spastics down to the Seaside. I, I recycle!
Alright – what do you do?

NAT: More than that.

TONY: Yeah – for drugs and Aids.

EMMA: Let's get him down to the club, your mum's going
to be worrying. We've got to go Tony.

TONY: Yeah about fucking time. I thought your arse was glued to that sofa, time it's spent there.

EMMA: You'd know, you've spent long enough staring at it.

TONY: No I ain't. Have I, have I Bill!

NAT: Don't drag him into it.

TONY: But I don't – I swear! Do I Bill.

BILLY: Constantly.

TONY: Alright that's it – out! You're kidding yourself love!

Enter CAROL – stage right.

CAROL: Stop shouting Tone.

TONY: Just accused me of staring at her arse? But I don't.

CAROL: We've got more important things to worry about. Don't bother about a solicitor.

TONY: When do I stare at her arse?

CAROL: When you're not staring at her tits.

TONY: No, no I don't. Solicitor? I've been trying but Kenny's phone's off.

CAROL: I know. I just been talking to him outside the nick. Him and Francis Smith.

TONY: What's Francis Smith got to do with it?

CAROL: For fucksake! Jamie's been nicked with that Chilli.

TONY: What, what happened to Trigger's –

CAROL: Jamie lied, he was meeting Chilli, to buy E's.

TONY: To buy! He's the victim here ain't he Nat. Buying them?

CAROL: He was going to sell them at the party!

TONY: Who's told you all this?

CAROL: Jamie. I just spoke to him through his cell window.

TONY: Oh my God – his cell window.

CAROL: He's fine.

TONY: Fine? He's going to get put away for this!

CAROL: Francis reckons –

TONY: I don't care what he fucking reckons!

CAROL: That Jamie'll get six months. Chilli's facing three years.

TONY: And?

CAROL: It's something they want to avoid.

TONY: Not at the expense of my son. What about his career? The BBC are sure to want a drug dealer jumping around on CBBC!

CAROL: Jamie wants to help. He's quite definite about that.

TONY: What are you smirking about?

NAT: Jamie's grasped the rudiments of the food chain then.

TONY: Her, her step father's on The Sunday Times Rich List!

CAROL: Straight?

EMMA: Under the circumstances Carol?

CAROL: Yeah.

BILLY: Thank God. Bye then.

Exit BILLY – stage right.

EMMA: I'll see you soon.

CAROL: No you won't. At least be straight about it Emma.

Exit EMMA – stage right.

TONY: Good luck with her mate. You're going to need it.

CAROL: Stop making a mug of yourself.

NAT: I hope things work out with your son.

CAROL: Yeah take care.

Exit NAT – stage right.

TONY: What a slag him? I'm going up there talk to Jamie.

CAROL: He's made his mind up Tony.

TONY: He'll go to prison – for something he's not done!

CAROL: Yeah but we can't bend the rules when it suits and go all squeaky when it don't.

TONY: I can when it's my son at stake.

CAROL: Our son.

TONY: He's been intimidated by the Smiths that's what it is.

CAROL: He ain't I just spoke to him!

TONY: I'll talk to the police then.

CAROL: And say what?

TONY: That Jamie was buying the stuff off Chilli.

CAROL: You'll grass?

TONY: Oh you can take the girl out of the Packington.

CAROL: At least I know right from wrong! You go up there and start bubbling people up Tone – you're on your own.

TONY: Jesus Carol – Jamie's about to chuck his life down the pan!

CAROL: He'll do a few months Youth Custody. Said yourself it'd do him good.

TONY: But…don't say much for our parenting skills this does it.

CAROL: Says a lot more than if he was in there squealing. Kenny reckons Detention Centre sorted him right out.

TONY: Kenny? He came from a problem family! Jamie's different.

CAROL: He's not! He's just another flash little fucker who wants to be one of the chaps.

TONY: What, what if I have a word with Kenny, negotiate a bit?

CAROL: There's nothing to negotiate. Anyway Kenny's not going to talk to you until he knows how you're going to shape.

TONY: I thought he was my mate? I remember the Smiths at Saturday morning pictures, bunking in. Jibbing into Saturday morning pictures! Urchins they were – urchins!

CAROL: Yeah well they're not now.

TONY: Fuck it they can shoot me then, they're not destroying my son's life.

CAROL: They ain't going to shoot you. They just won't like you. No one will.

TONY: So what?

CAROL: It spreads don't it. What's my mum and dad, my sister, done to be called grasses? People not trusting them?

TONY: I'm a taxpayer Carol. This gaff's worth over a million. Canonbury comes to another quarter. It's different around here now.

CAROL: It's still the Angel Tone.

TONY: I can't let this happen – honestly. If I was Nat you'd think I was a hero.

CAROL: But you're not are you. They got a solicitor, Sullivan. He's going to ring when he gets Jamie released.

TONY: Sullivan, knew it was something like that. Where you going?

CAROL: Down the Crown, see Tina and them.

TONY: Bollocks are you!

CAROL: Let go of me. I mean it Tony.

TONY: We're, we're in the middle of a crisis. You can't go now.

CAROL: Fucking watch me.

TONY: What about the Thai?

CAROL: (*Heading out.*) You eat it.

TONY: No, no wait – you're right. Do him good a bit of discipline. I won't say anything – honestly. Let's wait for the Thai eh?

CAROL: I'm not hungry anymore.

TONY: But, but –

CAROL: I want to go and have some fun Tony.

TONY: We will – honestly.

CAROL: Alone.

TONY: Alone?

CAROL: Without you. Without your involvement.

TONY: You want to, to go with other geezers?

CAROL: I don't know.

TONY: Just cos I – I wouldn't have done it. I wouldn't have said anything, wouldn't have grassed.

CAROL: It's not just that. Sullivan'll call when –

TONY: You want to perv over some fucking stripper?

CAROL: You've been perving over Emma for a fucking year!

TONY: No I haven't. I haven't – honestly. Carol we're happy. We're a happy family.

CAROL: I'm off.

TONY: You're coming back though aren't you – tonight?

CAROL: Not if you keep nagging.

TONY: What about Jamie?

CAROL: Give him the Thai.

TONY: No what shall I say about you?

CAROL: Tell him the truth.

TONY: He won't like that – honestly. You don't need to go off on your own – we can be swingers.

CAROL: Shut up! For once in your fucking life – be quiet.

CAROL prepares to leave.

TONY: Get them in the cab and that, career women – going out on their own. Lawyers, it's the same as that ain't it?

CAROL: These are pinching now. My feet don't stop spreading.

TONY: This just shows how strong our marriage is don't it.

CAROL: Don't wait up.

Exit CAROL – stage right.

Pause.

The phone rings.

TONY: Mr Sullivan? – Hello? – Sorry? – Oh yeah the Thai – What? – No it's number 44. I'll send someone to the door. Jamie you're going to wear through them football boots keep polishing them like that. He's mad about football my boy. Hang on. Alice! Is she still working on her thesis Jame? Hold on. Me wife's still in the shower. I tell you what, I'll meet you at the door. Here are mate, don't have a family, they're murder – honestly.

Exit TONY – stage right.

Lights down / music up.

The End.